Van Winkle's Return

Change in American
English, 1966–1986

Kenneth G. Wilson

Van Winkle's Return
Change in American English, 1966-1986

Published for University of Connecticut by
University Press of New England
Hanover and London, 1987

© 1987 by the Trustees of the University of Connecticut

Printed in the United States of America

LIBRARY OF CONGRESS CATALOGING-IN-PUBLICATION DATA

Wilson, Kenneth G. (Kenneth George), 1923–
Van Winkle's return.

Bibliography: p.
Includes index.
1. English language—United States—Variation.
2. English language—United States—Usage.
3. Americanisms.   4. English language—Social aspects—United States.   I. Title.
PE2808.W55   1987   428'.00973   86-40390
ISBN 0–87451–411–8
ISBN 0–87451–394–4 (pbk.)

To Marilyn

Contents

Acknowledgments

I'm very grateful to a good many people for their efforts, counsel, and encouragement while I was at work on this book: my students, colleagues, and friends; my editors, lexicographic acquaintances, and publishers; the members of the Editorial Committee of the University of Connecticut; and Charles Backus, Janice Bittner, Shirley Corcoran, Mary Crittendon, Irving Cummings, John Gatta, Julia Gatta, Walker Gibson, Kathryn Gohl, Michael Meyer, William Moynihan, Thomas Roberts, Milton Stern, Lois Torrence, and Marilyn Wilson.

To all, many, many thanks.

Storrs, Connecticut   K.G.W.
January 1987

Van Winkle's Return

Change in American
English, 1966–1986

CHAPTER 1

Introduction

During the first sixteen years of my working life, I studied, taught, and wrote about the English language. Then I wandered off and fell asleep: I became a college dean and a university vice president. (You will recall that Rip Van Winkle passed out after drinking immoderately of the powerful *genever* provided for the refreshment of Hendrick Hudson's bowling team; academic administration turned out to be pretty heady stuff too, and it diverted me a good deal longer than I'd planned.) Meantime, the English language went on changing, as language always does, and the study of language, the arguments about its use and abuse, and the efforts to understand, reform, liberate, preserve, modernize, regulate, correct, describe, and teach the English language went on apace without me.

Rip slept away twenty years, and his bewilderment at the world he found on waking has become a ready metaphor for the disorientation we all feel on returning to familiar scenes after long absence: while much looks the same, even more seems strange; some things are missing, others are unrecognizable, and still others, at first apparently unchanged, turn out after all not to be what they seem.

I was asleep to most of my former linguistic interests for about fifteen years, and I've taken another four or five to put myself back in the picture. That's roughly Rip's twenty years—almost a generation's worth of men, women, and children whose talking, listening, reading, and writing I failed to analyze at the time. Ever since 1966, when I drifted off, the language has continued to change, often without my noticing or having time to give it much attention. Yet my bewilderment on my return to my old trade, my old subject, and my old haunts has ended (with one exception: see chap. 14) in more interest than alarm: my confusions—and there have been many—have brought their delights too. Like before-and-after pictures of the same landscape, my observations of the English of the 1980s, superimposed on my recollections of the English of the 1960s, have highlighted the differences for me. Perhaps change stands out more clearly for me after my absence than it does for those who over those same years never took their ears and eyes off the language. At any rate, like Rip's absence, mine too stimulated my asking of questions and my seeking of explanations of puzzling new things I heard and saw. Change is the normal condition of a living language, but most of us live through change without noticing its tiny incremental processes; to be away for a time and then to return is to see those processes speeded up, as in time-lapse motion pictures of flowers opening.

The sixteen years I spent in teaching before my sleep were exciting times for any student of the English language. Following World War II there were fascinating developments and intense debates about most of them in nearly every facet of the study of language in general and of American English in particular. Consider the situation toward the end of that period, in the mid-1960s: a near revolution in the writing of English grammars was under way, the most notable developments being the maturing of structural grammars and the beginnings of transformational-generative and stratificational grammatical theory. There was a spate of new studies and compilations on various aspects of American English usage. Scholars were describing and accounting for more of the forms, causes, and effects of regional and social variation in our language. After the wartime hiatus, there was encouraging progress toward completion of the linguistic atlases of the United States and Canada (indeed, a good deal had been accomplished during the war), and linguistic geographers in this country were finally coming close to matching for American English the kinds of information Europeans had already compiled for some of their languages and dialects. The field of sociolinguistics, which examines the effects that social forces such as race or isolation can have on language, had developed considerable sophistication of procedure and was beginning to have an impact. In the public schools cocksure party lines on bilingualism for Hispanics and bidialectalism for English-speaking blacks were taking shape. The outrage over why Johnny couldn't read was being augmented with equally irate questions about why Johnny couldn't write, either. The censorship of school library books judged by parents and other vigilant citizens to contain obscene language was entering another rising phase in its frequently recurrent cycling.

In nearly every pure or applied field that treated of language—from engineering and education to philosophy and literature and linguistics itself—ferment seemed to characterize the mid-1960s. And the loudest and most publicly debated issue of all during this period was the long-drawn-out howl that marked the reception of the 1961 edition of *Webster's Third New International Dictionary of the English Language,* the G. and C. Merriam Company's monumental unabridged. Its publication elicited from reviewers in the popular press such heated arguments about the proper purposes of dictionaries that detailed scholarly reviews of the new book were deferred for some time while linguists and lexicographers wheeled their wagons into defensive circles against the attacks of larger numbers of ill-informed but righteously angry natives (some very distinguished tribal chiefs among them) than had been seen on the warpath for many years. All in all, when I left teaching in 1966, linguistics, lexicography, and nearly all aspects of the American English language itself were in a fine and lively uproar.

I probably missed a good deal of what went on in and around the language during the next fifteen years, but when bearded, beaded undergraduates—and sometimes their bearded, beaded teachers, too—shouted four-letter words at me for trying to prevent their intervening* in what they alleged were the university's complicities

---

*Here's a usage problem that most of the experts say is no longer an issue: the need for a genitive (possessive) case in the noun or pronoun preceding a gerund (or verbal noun). Some people would dodge the issue by writing *I tried to prevent them from intervening,* rather than choose either *to prevent their intervening* or *to prevent them intervening,* which uses the objective (accusative) case of the pronoun instead. In my sentence the *their* seemed the only thing to use, yet all around me I hear and frequently see *I don't like him driving so fast,* rather than *I don't like his driving so fast;* in the press we can frequently find things like *The regulars were opposed to Smith running for office,* rather than *Smith's running for office.* Note, however, that while the inflected noun is distinctively possessive in writing, in some instances speech doesn't always make the distinction possible (*Keats' spelling* and *Keats spelling* can be indistinguishable in speech). Among the pronouns the feminine singular affords no contrast, either; *I admire her acting* could be either possessive or objective case; we can't tell, as we can with *his acting* or *him acting* in a similar sentence.

Margaret Bryant (*Current American Usage*) reports on a series of studies of

in the machinations of the military-industrial complex, I got a fleeting but clear view of one sort of language change, stemming mainly from the Berkeley free speech movement and its easterly imitations. Of course I continued to use American English myself in my daily work, but I usually noticed new developments only by accident, as when I would observe a particularly curious usage, only to forget it before I could inquire into it, or when a language issue would leap for a time into the general public consciousness, thanks to a new book or essay or a newsworthy speech. I seldom looked into my scholarly journals, and, being an academic administrator, of course I rarely thought long or deeply about anything.

Oh, I did notice a few things. I read a few best-selling books on the language, such as Edwin Newman's two collections of examples of contemporary American English linguistic follies (*Strictly Speaking* and *A Civil Tongue*). I noted and to some extent shared Newman's concern for the future of the Republic should these follies continue unchecked. I saw that both Random House and American Heritage–Houghton Mifflin were putting out new dictionaries, the former probably and the latter avowedly dedicated to serving that right-thinking, clean-living band who were certain that *Webster III* (Merriam's 1961 edition of its unabridged, *Webster's Third New International Dictionary*) was permissive and therefore wholly pernicious. I heard too that Oxford University Press would soon publish a dictionary of American English— perhaps because Americans had been unable to do it properly for themselves. And I read that the first two volumes had appeared of what is now a completed four-volume second supplement to the great *Oxford English Dictionary*.

From time to time I noted the well-meant but probably misguided efforts of supporters of bilingualism and bidialectalism in

---

twenty-five and more years ago: "In written formal English, both nouns and pronouns almost always occur in the genitive case before a gerund" (51). Note the *almost*. But by 1974, in the second edition of the study he wrote for the National Council of Teachers of English (*The Teaching of English Usage*), the late Robert C. Pooley advised "that the following eight items need no longer be 'corrected' in the classroom and that these forms are acceptable to many educated speakers and writers today." The eighth item in Pooley's list is "Any insistence upon the possessive case standing before a gerund" (209). My prose in this instance seems to reflect the tastes of a conservative last leaf.

the schools, and without enough information of my own about what actions were actually being taken, I worried briefly at what appeared to be the great weaknesses some of these evangelicals revealed in their knowledge of how language really works; I was unhappy about the almost certain damage to minority children should some of these proposals become policy. I heard too about major new developments in grammatical theory, noting that here and there in the intersections between psycholinguistics and philosophy, inquirers were addressing perhaps the most interesting questions of all, those concerning the universals of language and the genetic aspects of our innate "knowledge" of grammar. I noted the growing interest in semiotics (a theory of signs and symbols), which from my ill-informed distance looked suspiciously like a new, wide-spectrum wonder drug being marketed to treat the indispositions of intellectuals. I learned from the grapevine that more of the linguistic atlas materials had been published, and I heard rumors that the long-awaited *Dictionary of American Regional English** was at last nearly ready to begin publication. Both these developments promised that we might soon know even more about our regional American dialectal variations than we have ever known before. I dutifully shelved the new fascicles of the *Middle English Dictionary* as they came in the mail, observing that the book had finally reached the letter *R,* and learning too that its fourth editor in chief had retired and that editor number five was now on the job. And, like nearly everyone else, I enjoyed the growing number of newspaper Safires who sparkled for themselves and for the rest of us by collecting and displaying some of the vagaries of current American usage, spoken and written.

Of course I criticized others' language and my own, being mordantly amused at the flatulent prose of many of my academic colleagues and at the syntactic and lexical follies of the Secretary Haigs and other public persons who brutalized the language daily, either because they could not use it clearly or because they dared not. I was only partly amused at some of the new instances of euphemism and doublespeak displayed by leaders in government and business in their unceasing efforts to improve or conceal some

*The first volume, letters A–C, appeared in late 1985.

of the uglier features of politics and the economy. And I was nearly always diverted by the language of advertising.

When, like Rip, I stumbled back into my old environment, I found that both it and I had changed. Of Rip, Washington Irving remarks, "As he rose to walk, he found himself stiff in the joints, and wanting in his usual activity" (59). I too was rusty and out of date. So were most of my desk dictionaries, and now there were some new ones to be mastered. Stacks of books and journals, some of them more than a decade old, were waiting to be read; their titles promised important discoveries, new departures, remarkable conclusions never heretofore deemed possible, and many other proofs that revolutions had occurred while I slept. The prospect of ever catching up was daunting; it appeared likely that the changes in some aspects of the language, in our knowledge of it, and in our attitudes toward it, might be as sweeping as those that so shook Rip when he identified himself to the curious villagers as a loyal subject of good King George and found himself accused of treasonable Tory talk against a President Washington.

So I went about trying to catch up. What follows here is an account of what I found out. Here, as I return to teaching and writing about the language, are my informal observations on some aspects of the present state of American English and our current opinions of it, as compared with the way I thought I had left these matters in 1966. I'm writing not for a scholarly audience but for lay people who are curious about their language, for amateurs of language who love the stuff. I've written few footnotes, and most of them are comments on usage items that turn up in my own prose. I don't try to reach final conclusions on whether my students, or Americans in general, are more sophisticated in their views of the language today than they were twenty years ago. Such matters seem to me too complex for easy generalization just yet. Rather, this book is an impressionistic view, not a systematic one. What I consider the most important developments and changes since 1966 may not be the ones my colleagues who never slept would select. But this is what the forest and some of its trees look like to me on my return. I may well be slighting or overlooking some interesting groves and important thickets and even some individual forest giants, but the matters with which I deal here seem to me to be the important ones. I think these observations on trees and forest point up much of what has happened to American English and to our views of it over the twenty years just past. A Van Winkle's observations are not likely to be wise, but they *are* responses to real stimuli, and, just as in Rip's case, so in this one: the wise reader may see even more than the awakened sleeper himself understands.

CHAPTER 2

The "Big" Dictionary: The Standards
of *Webster III*

I started out with dictionaries when I got back. The changes in language most of us notice first are usually changes in vocabulary—changes in words: their meanings, their pronunciations, and their shifts in status. So it was with me when I began to try to catch up. The way to keep track of changes in vocabulary, of course, is to listen and read and then consult the dictionaries. And for keeping up with current American English, the dictionaries to consult are the college desk dictionaries. Our unabridged "big" dictionaries are wonderful books, influential, widely available, and stuffed with lore, but no general dictionaries are more useful for finding out about the *current* vocabulary than the fine American "college" dictionaries. To explain how they got that way, however, I need first to say a bit about the "big" books—the unabridged dictionaries, especially *Webster III*, Merriam's *Webster's Third New International* (1961). *Webster III* leads not just to change in the language, but to change in the way dictionaries record it, and change in our attitudes toward it as well.

American dictionary-making has long been of very high quality. American lexicographers have been producing fine scholarly dictionaries of various kinds, and they have also been turning out excellent commercial dictionaries for both general and special purposes, dictionaries that are *commercial* in that they are designed to make money for their publishers. And make money they do.

In the 1960s, however, American lexicographers were embroiled with dictionary reviewers, buyers, and users in arguments about permissiveness and other sins, arguments of an intensity and vituperation unmatched in the trade since the Webster-Worcester dictionary wars of the nineteenth century. (Joseph Worcester worked on Noah Webster's dictionaries and later gave them vigor-

8

ous competition with books of his own; Webster and his heirs were
not pleased.) In the 1960s the arguments centered primarily on the
big commercial books, not the scholarly ones, and the main issue
was an old, oversimple question: should the dictionary maker just
describe the vocabulary, or should he also or instead *prescribe* it?
That is, should the lexicographer tell the user how to decide what
to say or write in a particular situation, or should he simply tell the
user what is right?

As it's turned out, this still-raging argument has worked to every
dictionary user's advantage. For more than two decades, as reviewers have argued about the right purposes for dictionaries, many
general readers have developed a considerable interest in the question, an interest that has by no means faded today. And above all,
the fierce competition for increasingly profitable dictionary markets, especially the college student market, has obliged publishers
to produce new and revised dictionaries of steadily improving
quality at increasingly frequent intervals and at relatively unchanged prices. Given the differing tastes within these growing
markets, the good dictionaries have developed along somewhat
different lines, as each publisher has decided which tastes to woo.
What had been a very healthy* situation for the dictionary buyer
and the dictionary user since the end of World War II has over the
past twenty years become even healthier. How did it all come
about? We'll begin with the "big" dictionaries.

From 1934 to 1961 the most widely used unabridged commercial dictionary in the United States was *Webster's New International Dictionary of the English Language,* second edition (hereafter, *Webster II*), published in 1934 by the G. and C. Merriam
Company of Springfield, Massachusetts. Merriam, of course,
made much of the fact that it had long been publisher of Noah

---

*A few conservatives may object that *healthful* is the term I should have used
here. *Webster III* (1961), in its synonymy on *healthful,* comments, "HEALTHFUL and
HEALTHY are both used to mean conducive to or indicative of health or soundness,
the former word being preferred [in these senses] in some quarters." The usage note
at the *healthy* entry in *American Heritage II* (1982), the most conservative of the
good current college dictionaries, says, "One can expect to be *healthy* ('full of
health') if the regimen one follows is *healthful* ('conducive to health'). However, the
distinction is breaking down." *Healthful* is largely restricted to the meaning "conducive to health," but *healthy* is commonly used in both senses: *a healthy person; a
healthy climate.* Or, as I have used it, *a healthy situation.* Twenty years ago, I'd have
written *healthful,* but this time, without hesitation, I didn't.

Webster's dictionaries and that this one was the direct descendant of the great man's own dictionaries. By the end of World War II, most of *Webster II*'s early competition had gone either out of date or out of business. The great multivolumed *Century Dictionary and Cyclopedia*, edited by Yale's William Dwight Whitney and published by the Century Company in 1899, had gone through a number of printings around the turn of the century, but it was no longer in print. Funk and Wagnalls, which continued to sell dictionaries and which remained a household word at least through the 1960s (remember television's "Laugh-In" program, with its "Look *that* up in your Funk and Wagnalls!"), had put its *New Standard Dictionary*, first published in 1913, through many printings and editions; but the Funk and Wagnalls dictionaries were losing out to the Merriam books in the postwar years, at least in scholarly reputation, mainly because Funk and Wagnalls had taken to revising only infrequently and minimally. The *New Standard* or one of its several offspring* could still be bought in the early 1960s in a variety of formats as premiums in supermarkets and as tie-in bonuses for purchasers of encyclopedias. After 1934, at first gradually and then rapidly, it ceased to be serious competition as an authoritative unabridged book, particularly for scholars and other professionals.

Of course there were other unabridged dictionaries around in 1961 when Merriam published *Webster III*. The great *Oxford English Dictionary* (hereafter, *OED*) was still unchallenged, as it had been since its completion in 1928 and as it still is today, for its historical record of the English vocabulary. But the *OED* was primarily a scholar's, not a layman's book, particularly in the United States. Its size, its cost, and its nationality all worked against its popular use in this country. It was published in thirteen large, heavy volumes; it was very expensive; it recorded only British pronunciations, and not a great many of those; and without its 1933 supplement, it covered the language only up through the 1920s for the latter part of the alphabet and through the beginning

---

*In *its several offspring*, the noun is clearly an s-less plural. But I'm pretty sure I've heard *offsprings* too, although the word sounds odd to me. Merriam's *Ninth New Collegiate*, *Random House Revised*, and *New World II*, three of today's big four college dictionaries, all report both plurals: *offspring* and *offsprings*, in that order and with no usage notes. *American Heritage II* declines to go along; it recognizes only one plural, *offspring*. Here, it seems, I followed conservative practice.

of the twentieth century for the earlier letters. For American users the *OED* was rarely helpful for the contemporary language, particularly for American versions of it. At best the supplement covered the vocabulary through the 1920s. Its spellings were British, not American, and everyone knew that there were differences. Some American Anglophiles preferred the two-volume *Shorter Oxford Dictionary*, an abridgement of the *OED*, but although the *Shorter Oxford* served purposes and markets in England and the Commonwealth countries somewhat similar to those served by *Webster II* in the United States, it could provide Americans with neither all the kinds of lexicographic information nor most of the encyclopedic material they had come to expect to find in their "big" dictionaries. And even though it was large, the *Shorter Oxford* was an abridgement and a British one at that; that its language wasn't American English was a bigger drawback than some of its American users realized.

I've already mentioned the *Century* and Funk and Wagnalls' *New Standard*. Although the *Century* in particular was an admirable achievement and was still much praised and used by scholars for some purposes in the 1960s (it had superb definitions, perhaps the best ever written for much of the language, and it was undoubtedly the best encyclopedic dictionary ever produced in this country), neither it nor the *New Standard* was any longer a *current* dictionary.

In 1961 there was one fairly recent unabridged dictionary to compete with the newly published *Webster III*: World Publishing Company's *Webster's New World Dictionary*, encyclopedic edition, which had appeared in 1951 and had gone through at least four more printings by 1957. This book appears not seriously to have reduced *Webster II*'s share of the market for unabridged dictionaries in the 1950s, however, and until 1961 Merriam seemed still to have the field pretty much to itself. But the college market was a different story. Moreover, by winning in the courts the decision that the Webster name was no longer Merriam's exclusive property, World did indeed discomfit Merriam. But its unabridged book, although it appears to have sold well at first, seems not to have affected Merriam's grip on the market for "big" dictionaries. Only later, when it put out its college book, did World appear to affect Merriam.

At any rate, until 1961 *Webster II* was essentially *the* one-volume, encyclopedic, unabridged general dictionary in America. It was used almost everywhere, even in the courts, to settle questions of meaning, pronunciation, spelling, syllabication, etymology, and status and appropriateness of use. "The dictionary," when an unabridged was called for, was usually *Webster II.* "Webster says" nearly always meant *Webster II,* court decision or not.

But when, almost a full generation after *Webster II* first appeared, Merriam published *Webster III* (full title: *Webster's Third New International Dictionary of the English Language*), the uproar was immediate and prodigious. This occurred in 1961, and for at least the next decade the Republic was ablaze with controversy over *Webster III*—over the propriety of its purposes, the integrity of its methods, the quality of its judgments, the utility of its format, and the implications of the book for the future of the language and the good of the community it was intended to serve. At the very least, many people were unhappy simply because it was different from *Webster II*; others—a large and very vocal group—insisted that it was downright dangerous.

For many it was as though someone had rewritten the King James Version of the Bible or the *Book of Common Prayer* in words taken from the walls of the men's room; "they" were destroying all standards of decency and rectitude, tampering with tradition, tinkering with truth. The publication of *Webster III* in 1961 caused an explosion. Few books lacking argument, characters, and plot (although some reviewers were certain that there was a plot behind it all) have ever created a greater or longer-lasting furor, both critical and popular.

First the editorial pages of the major national newspapers and then of the weeklies and monthlies lambasted the book, the Merriam Company, linguistics, linguists, lexicographers generally, and Merriam's editor in chief, the late Philip B. Gove, in particular. Later, when the scholarly journals got into the fray, most of them defended some or even most of the changes the editors of *Webster III* had adopted for the new edition. There is little need to go into great detail here; the whole noisy argument has been splendidly documented in James Sledd and Wilma R. Ebbitt's *Dictionaries and THAT Dictionary* (1962). Among the charges leveled were these: the format was new and unfamiliar, and some of the space-saving devices it employed made *Webster III* seem harder to use than *Webster II* had been. The *colloquial* status label had been dropped and not replaced by any other sort of label. This change alone was a major issue: there were many words that in 1934's *Webster II* had carried *colloquial* or even *slang* labels that now, in 1961's *Webster III*, on the strength of a full generation's new citations, carried no label at all. Such changes led some hasty judges to conclude, quite wrongly, that the new book had dropped *all* standards of usage and all of the labels that in the old book had tagged words and senses thought to be of limited acceptability at that time. Some of the citations bothered some reviewers: a best-seller by the madam of a New York whorehouse, Polly Adler's *A House Is Not a Home*, was deemed an unworthy source for citation, as were at one point or another nearly all our major newspapers and magazines, including *Life, Time*, and the *New York Times*. Reviewers who were accustomed apparently to having their dictionaries cite only distinguished dead English and American authors, whether these were still being widely read or not, violently opposed *Webster III*'s citations of language from the business, sports, and news columns of metropolitan daily newspapers and from national magazines, to say nothing of the even more earthy language of some contemporary American fiction, drama, and poetry.

Further, because it needed more space for the vocabulary yet had to stay within the limitations of a one-volume format and a reasonable purchase price, *Webster III* omitted much of the encyclopedic information *Webster II* had provided: the names, dates, and occupations of famous people in history, the names of cities and countries with their populations and square mileage, and a range of other helpful lore that *Webster II* had included either in its main alphabet or in its many pages of "Pronouncing Gazetteer" and "Pronouncing Biographical Dictionary" at the end of the book. Some people did not like the new system *Webster III* used to represent pronunciations, or the layout, typography, and abbreviations used in the definitions, and nearly everybody damned the dropping of the pronunciation key from the bottom of each page. But most of all, nearly everyone who didn't like the book came back to one devastating fault: the book was permissive: it did not tell the reader what was right. It included words and meanings that nice people shouldn't use, and it failed to warn the unwary that many words and meanings that might indeed exist ought not to and should therefore certainly be avoided if not suppressed from the book altogether.

Perhaps the whole issue can most briefly be summarized for my purposes here in two quotations from the time, quotations that suggest both the substance of the quarrel (where there *was* substance) and the high emotional pitch of much of the argument.

First, Sumner Ives, an American professor of English, writing a review in the journal *Word Study*:

This latest dictionary . . . is an intellectual achievement of the very highest order. . . . To the scholar in language, who knows something of the difficulties in such a project, the consistent skill which has been displayed is most impressive. To one who simply wishes to use a dictionary, it is of primary importance that this dictionary . . . embodies the best and most thoroughly established principles of current scholarship in language, and that it is based on the largest available collection of evidence showing what current English usage actually is. Whatever authority these attributes give, it has. (8)

And then in a piece called "Sabotage in Springfield," here is Wilson Follett, writing in *The Atlantic*:

Webster III, behind its front of passionless objectivity, is in truth a fighting document. And the enemy it is out to destroy is every obstinate vestige of linguistic punctilio, every surviving influence that makes for the upholding of standards, every criterion for distinguishing between better usages and worse. In other words, it has gone over bodily to the school that construes traditions as enslaving, the rudimentary principles of syntax as crippling, and taste as irrelevant. (73)

Pretty strong stuff, that. Like Follett, many others were most unhappy with *Webster III*, or at least with whatever purported samples of its contents they saw or heard about when the book first appeared. At least one major newspaper plunged its head in the sand and declared editorially that everyone should stick with the old *Webster II*, ignoring the fact that several of the horrible examples the editorial writer cited from *Webster III* were essentially unchanged from the entries he would have found had he actually consulted *Webster II* (*Washington Post*, 17 January 1962, A14).

Linguists and lexicographers fought back, most of them clearly on the defensive, nearly all of them outraged at what they considered the know-nothing attitudes of the popular reviewers. It was to be several years before scholarly reviewers got around to detailed criticism of *Webster III* themselves, so sweeping were the attacks by those who hated it and who would not listen to those who pointed out that the book had been put together on mostly the same sound principles that lexicographers had long been using. *Webster III* was seen to describe without prescribing, and "permissiveness" was its fatal flaw, along with its recording of changes in the language that many commentators did not want to admit had taken place or believed ought not to have taken place.

Of course *Webster III* was not a failure, and it is today very widely used, and justifiably so. Its editors had made some editorial choices and compromises to which critics and linguistic scholars still take exception, but on the whole the book is sound, and the information it contains is remarkably accurate; some of its information about American English can be found nowhere else. But there is no question that when it was launched twenty-five years ago, *Webster III* had rough sailing. As a consequence, the dictionary industry was much stimulated, speeded up, and put on its mettle. Publishers' hearts leaped up at the thought of a hitherto unassailable competitor vulnerable at last; they rubbed their hands at the thought of profitable new markets for their own wares. Lexicography itself came under wider and more direct public and scholarly scrutiny than it had undergone for many years—perhaps ever. Competition grew rapidly in the trade, as other dictionaries were made that tried to respond directly—in format and editorial policy—to many of the criticisms leveled at *Webster III*. All this has made the twenty years between the mid-1960s and today an unusually lively period for dictionaries, for their editors and publishers, and for their buyers and users.

For one thing, the dissatisfaction with *Webster III* so loudly voiced in the early 1960s led very quickly to the publication of some fine new dictionaries, among them a new unabridged American book, the *Random House Dictionary of the English Language*, which appeared in 1966. And there was also a new desk dictionary, *The American Heritage Dictionary of the English Language*, which was published by American Heritage and Houghton Mifflin Company in 1969. Both were very good dictionaries, although very different in purpose, size, and scope; both were direct responses to the market that had declared itself dissatisfied with *Webster III*.

The unabridged *Random House*'s lexicography was by no means reactionary, and it quickly found favor with many readers, some of whom no doubt chose it simply because it wasn't *Webster III*. But they too soon came to realize that it was indeed a solid modern unabridged, perhaps not so large and all encompassing in its vocabulary as *Webster III*, but more generous in its use of status labels, more traditional in its inclusion of encyclopedic information, and more familiar looking in format. By 1979 Random House's unabridged had gone through seven printings; it was the first all-new American unabridged commercial dictionary since 1934 to win—partly as a book club premium—a significant share of the market for "big" dictionaries.

Although I'll discuss it in the next chapter with the other college books, I mention *The American Heritage Dictionary* here because it was not at first aimed at the college market. Rather, it was at first a new desk-sized dictionary aimed explicitly at the segment of the literate general public that wanted conservative advice on usage: the older generations and their friends. It was a well-edited, handsomely printed (in larger type and in a larger page format than most desk dictionaries), strikingly illustrated book, using almost no abbreviations in its entries. In every way possible, it tried to respond to the criticisms leveled at *Webster III*. It probably claimed a good deal more for its aging panel of advisers on usage than their contributions warranted even in 1969, but it left no one in doubt about what it thought was *right*. It could not compete for completeness with *Webster III* or with Random House's unabridged, or World's, or anyone else's; it was far too small for that. In cost and general purpose it was much more likely to compete with the college dictionaries, and, as we shall see, that is what it came ultimately to do.

One other new dictionary requires a brief notice here, even if only to make clear that it is not comparable to the good college books I'll be discussing from here on. In 1980 Oxford University Press in New York published *The Oxford American Dictionary*, an oversimple, ultraconservative desk dictionary with a vocabulary about half the size of that found in most other college desk dictionaries, but with a price almost exactly like theirs. About half its many usage notes read like this informative one for *disguise*: "Do not confuse *disguise* with *guise.*" Or consider the inaccurate picture its note on *disinterested* provides: "Careful writers regard the second use [uninterested, uncaring] as unacceptable because it obscures a useful distinction between *disinterested* and *uninterested.*" Alas, nearly all other current desk dictionaries make it very clear that this distinction is a very complex matter, as I'll demonstrate in chapter 13. The truth is that there is better lexicographical information in most four-to-eight-dollar paperback "pocket" dictionaries than there is in the *Oxford American Dictionary*—a poor, unworthy, distant American relative of the great *OED*.

At any rate, in the 1960s the world of lexicography was aboil, and professional and lay people alike were deeply engaged. The catalyst was Merriam's *Webster III*, an unabridged, but in the end it was the college desk dictionaries, which had been in a flurry of growth and change ever since the end of World War II, that changed the most over those twenty years. Partly, of course, it was because these dictionaries could report the changes in language most quickly of all general dictionaries, and partly it was a change in market that made the difference. But the fact is that in editorial and marketing philosophy as well as in format and content, the college dictionaries in the 1980s reflected some marked changes in American attitudes toward the language.

CHAPTER 3

The Great College Dictionary Race

Why start with the college dictionaries? How could they help put me back into the picture? Because they record what's going on in the vocabulary more promptly than do other general dictionaries: they pick up new or variant spellings, pronunciations, meanings, combined forms, and usage judgments. And because their new printings and new editions appear so frequently, they can almost always note such changes earlier and more sensitively than can the unabridged dictionaries, whose new editions are likely to come out only once a generation at best. Then, too, the college books' changing editorial policies clearly mirror our changing attitudes toward the language and toward other manners.

The greatest activity in American lexicography since World War II—and especially since the 1960s—has involved the college dictionaries, those one-volume, desk-sized dictionaries so peculiarly American. They are perhaps the most remarkable achievement of twentieth-century American dictionary-making. Other modern languages simply don't have exactly this sort of book, although some imitations are beginning to appear abroad. But like Noah Webster's *Spelling-Book* and the McGuffey readers, the college dictionaries are uniquely ours.

They have three main virtues: they're inexpensive, they're portable, and above all, they're current. Although they can't possibly cover as much of the vocabulary as a *Webster III* can, they do contain a very high percentage of the current vocabulary—more than most people would suspect. They usually have a good deal of encyclopedic information, listed either in separate alphabets at the end of the book or in the single main alphabet with all the other entries. The separate alphabets are the Merriam format and now, after a change, also *American Heritage*'s. The single alphabet for everything is a format used by some of the other leaders in the field today; it was pioneered in 1947 by Random House's splendid but now-defunct *American College Dictionary*, of which I'll have more to say a bit later on.

But the most important of all their virtues is the fact that college dictionaries are the most up-to-date general dictionaries we have: because every college student is expected to own one, and because they cost so little (less than most hardback trade books today), they have built a large and profitable market, one of the most lucrative in all of publishing, and so can revise fully and frequently. It could well be said that Merriam's collegiate series, especially its fifth edition, affected the college dictionary business the way Henry Ford's Model T—the "Tin Lizzie"—affected the automobile business. From the *Fifth* on, collegiate dictionary publishing has been big, BIG business.

Today, competition among college dictionaries is so strong that it keeps prices low and quality high. The best of these books come out in new editions increasingly often, and because of their high sales volume they are frequently reprinted between editions, usually with modest updating of entries or parts of entries; most recently, the leaders in the field have been reprinted nearly every year. This increased frequency of new editions and new printings means that new words, new status labels, and changing meanings and pronunciations can be kept more nearly up to the minute than those in any unabridged dictionary. Given the monumental size and cost of the task, the revising of unabridged dictionaries is comparatively infrequent; the twenty-seven years between *Webster II* and *Webster III* has been typical of the best. It's been twenty-five years since *Webster III* appeared, whereas *Webster's Ninth New Collegiate* followed the *Eighth* after just ten years. So I used the college dictionaries as an excellent and convenient way to check my observations and intuitions about the changes I thought I was seeing and hearing in the language. But I found too that the dictionaries themselves had changed: both their word lists and their editorial policies seemed to reflect some important shifts in our attitudes toward the language.

How did the college books become so important? It's worth a very brief look at their recent history to see how they have become so useful for my purposes—and lots of others. We all consult the college dictionaries, but few of us really know much about them.

Beginning in 1936 with the publication of its *Webster's Collegiate Dictionary*, fifth edition, Merriam had the college market
well in hand for many years. It shared some of that market with *The
Winston Dictionary*, published in Philadelphia from 1926 through
World War II, and with one or another Funk and Wagnalls
printing, but by the time the United States entered the war,
Merriam's *Fifth Collegiate* had control of the college dictionary
market. Winston hadn't kept up; perhaps its handicap was the lack
of a bellwether unabridged of the stature of Merriam's *Webster II*
on which to base its abridgment; perhaps Merriam's reminding
everyone that it had a staff in being continuously, not just when
doing a new edition or printing, made the difference; whatever the
reasons, Merriam increased its domination of the college market.
Its sales were promoted by a staff of college travelers, and its
adoptions were reflected in and no doubt influenced by its distribution of large numbers of free desk copies bearing the names of the
instructors printed in gold on the covers; these could be found on
nearly every English teacher's desk on nearly every campus in the
land. The *Fifth Collegiate* was a good book, well edited, and based
on the best unabridged then available, *Webster II*.

But Merriam continued to market its *Fifth* until 1948, a twelve-
year run that no college dictionary could easily survive today. The
rapid increase in the pace of producing new editions is one of the
radical changes that have taken place in these past twenty years.

Merriam had reprinted the *Fifth* many times, making modest
changes to bring new words into the main word list, usually
without having to reset many pages; if a new word or a new
meaning had to be entered, the usual procedure was to drop or
reduce an entry or two somewhere close by and then squeeze the
new item into the vacated space. At most, they'd reset a column or
a page. Gazetteer and biographical sections were separate in the
Merriam book, so these could be reset inexpensively (as compared
with the cost of resetting the whole book) to permit a new printing
to accommodate current census figures, new names, and recent
death dates.

Immediately after World War II, when the colleges and universities overflowed with returning veterans, many of whom might
never have attended college or bought dictionaries had it not been
for the G.I. Bill, the market for college dictionaries, like the mar-

ket for college textbooks, simply exploded. Publishers responded quickly. In 1947 two new dictionaries aimed directly at that market were published: Funk and Wagnalls' *New College Standard Dictionary*, which was essentially a revision of its old *Practical "Standard,"* and Random House's brand new *American College Dictionary* (hereafter, *ACD*), which turned out to be one of the all-time best and most influential of college dictionaries. *ACD* appeared to have based many of its definitions on those of the fine old *Century*. Its several new features were extremely well received: it entered gazetteer, abbreviations, biographical names, and other encyclopedic lore in the main alphabet, right along with the rest of the vocabulary. It chose its words and ordered the meanings within entries on the basis of "frequency of use," a policy designed to present the most current common meaning of the word first, and more specialized, arcane, or archaic meanings toward the end of the entry. It based its decisions on how to order its meanings partly on some statistical studies of the language, but even more on editorial judgment. But the big change was using "frequency of use," however arrived at, instead of an historical order, oldest meaning first, such as Merriam and most other dictionary makers had used for many years to set the order of meanings within an entry. *ACD's* avowed purpose was to serve the user's convenience and not to require him to read the whole entry to find what he wanted.

So, for example, in *Fifth Collegiate's* entry for *nice*, the most common definition, "pleasing; agreeable" was number 8; in *ACD* this most common, current sense was number 1 in the entry; the *Fifth's* first definition for *nice* was "*obs.* a. Foolish; silly. b. Lewd; wanton." In *ACD* "*Obs* wanton" was definition 14, "*obs* foolish" definition 15. The *Fifth* put the etymology immediately after the pronunciation and part-of-speech label, right near the head of the entry; *ACD* put the etymology at the very end of the entry.

Everything about the *ACD* was designed to promote ease of use; it adopted a large boldface type for the entry word itself (as did Funk and Wagnalls' *New College Standard*). *ACD* also pioneered the use of the International Phonetic Alphabet's symbol *schwa* [ə] to record unstressed vowels in its pronunciations (el ′əfənt) (sō′də)— a first for commercial dictionaries intended for the general public. All in all, *ACD* was a fine, high-quality dictionary, well edited, energetically advertised and merchandised, and very favorably reviewed. It was quickly and widely adopted in the college market, and its features were subsequently imitated by much of the competition.

Funk and Wagnalls' new book made no particular splash in the college market in 1947. I doubt it would have made much headway against Merriam's *Fifth Collegiate* in any case, but *ACD* was such a smash hit that the *New College Standard* went relatively unnoticed in academe. By 1958, in the still-growing market which the *Fifth Collegiate* had dominated for so long, the new *ACD* had gone through at least twelve printings and had won a large share of what had hitherto been Merriam's turf alone. One investment wonder of the mid-1950s was the New Jersey Turnpike; so successful had that new toll road been that its bonds paid off in record time, far more quickly than anyone had predicted. In the book business, Random House's large investment in *ACD* won a similar reputation: in the bookmen's bars along Third Avenue, you could hear publishing people marveling over their martinis that *ACD* had paid off "even faster than the Jersey Turnpike!"

Merriam responded to the competition, of course, and brought out its *Webster's New Collegiate Dictionary*, sixth edition, in 1949, just two years after the appearance of *ACD* and *New College Standard*. It stuck to its historical order of senses within entries, however, as it did to its use of separate alphabets for gazetteer and biographicals. But the *Sixth New Collegiate* was fully revised, a completely new edition.

Then in 1953 another new college dictionary appeared: World Publishing Company's *Webster's New World Dictionary*, college edition. Unlike *ACD*, which was an entirely new book and stood pretty much on its own, the *New World* was based on its parent unabridged, *Webster's New World Dictionary*, encyclopedic edition, published just two years before, in 1951. World, having won the right to use the Webster name, much to Merriam's dismay and the layman's confusion, produced a new college book that was also very well done and very well received; it went through eight printings in the eight years between 1953 and 1960, and it won its own respectable share of the ever-growing college market. It appeared to have learned some of its tricks from *ACD* (everything on one alphabet and the schwa for unstressed vowels, for example), and it added a few more of its own. Among college teachers it had a reputation for including more of the colloquial vocabulary and more current slang (all of course carefully labeled) than did the competition.

In 1961 came the unabridged *Webster III*, which Merriam followed in 1963 with a new college book based on it: *Webster's Seventh New Collegiate Dictionary*. The *Fifth Collegiate* had held the field for twelve years; the *Sixth New Collegiate*, with which in 1949 Merriam had countered *ACD*'s 1947 success, had lasted for fourteen years; now, however, the competition was too strong for even as fine a book as *ACD* to play much longer with a pat hand.

Then in 1963, Harcourt, Brace and World, Inc., joined forces with Funk and Wagnalls to produce another new book for the college market: the *Funk and Wagnalls Standard College Dictionary* (hereafter, *SCD*). It was Funk and Wagnalls' first new approach to the college market since 1947, and it had the advantage of Harcourt, Brace and World's large textbook operation to merchandise it in the colleges; Funk and Wagnalls had not worked the colleges well for many years.

But *Webster III* had made a great many people very unhappy indeed. *Seventh New Collegiate* of course perpetuated a lot of *Webster III*'s qualities, and so more new dictionaries were being prepared, books intended to satisfy the dissatisfied, to meet directly some of the louder criticisms aimed at the new Merriam unabridged. And, by no means incidentally, these new books hoped to win from the *Seventh* a share of the still-expanding market for college dictionaries—now more profitable than ever for those who could succeed in it.

So, when I left teaching in 1966, there were four good college dictionaries on my table: the nineteen-year-old *ACD*, whose share of the market had been much reduced by then, both because of the competition and because the book had not been fully revised; that it had lasted so long was evidence of its original quality and its popularity during the 1950s; the three-year-old *Seventh New Collegiate*, based on a strong but very controversial unabridged; the thirteen-year-old *New World*, still in its first edition but holding a reasonable share of the college market; and the three-year-old *SCD*, being heavily promoted but with no real track record. Also in 1966 Random House published its new unabridged, and the report was that there would shortly be a new college edition based on it—perhaps a revised *ACD*, perhaps a new book entirely. Still another report said that American Heritage and Houghton Mifflin were at work on a completely new dictionary, not necessarily for the college market, but for everyone who hated *Webster III*.

In 1968 came the *Random House College Dictionary*, followed in 1969 by the new *American Heritage Dictionary of the English Language*, which after an almost instant critical and sales success was reissued for the college market, reprinted in a format slightly reduced in page and print size, but unchanged in content; this latter edition was renamed *The American Heritage Dictionary*, college edition. The others—or most of them—responded: in 1970 came the second college edition of *New World*, *New World II*, this one published by Simon and Schuster instead of World Publishing.

Merriam countered in 1973 with another *Webster's New Collegiate Dictionary*, identified in the front matter but not on the title page as the eighth edition in the firm's *Collegiate* series. This time Merriam had let only ten years elapse before issuing a new edition. And the pace continued to accelerate: in 1975, after just seven years with its first edition, Random House published the revised edition of its college book.

The next move came from American Heritage and Houghton Mifflin: the second college edition, *American Heritage II*, appeared in 1982, and it in turn was followed in 1983 by still another Merriam *New Collegiate*, the *Ninth*. Today, of the good college dictionaries, only *New World II* is more than nine years old, *ACD* having been replaced by *Random House* and then by *Random House Revised*, and *SCD* having dropped into relative obscurity after being moved from Harcourt Brace Jovanovich to Harper and Row. The book now has a new name—*Funk and Wagnalls Standard Desk Dictionary*—and will apparently no longer compete in the fastest of all the fast lanes in dictionary publishing, that of the college dictionaries.

Merriam's *Fifth Collegiate* had lasted twelve years and had done superbly well throughout most of that span. But so brisk did the market become after the mid-1960s that, for the four best college dictionaries on my table in 1985, the average time since their previous editions was between six and seven years. That, or something under a decade at most, seems to be the limit today for a college dictionary if it's to stay current and compete. Like Olympic hopefuls, they all must run faster these days, or not at all. Everything else equal, youth in a college dictionary is the key; without current information, a college dictionary gives away the best of its three reasons for being. Inexpensive, portable, but out of date does not describe a successful dictionary for the college market.

So the past twenty years have seen a big change in the way college dictionaries are produced and sold. The catalysts were ACD and *Webster III*. Some of the merchandising has been almost comical: in 1981, for example, when I bought new current editions, I found that of the top four, all but *New World II* were being sold in red cloth hardcovers with gold lettering, bright red dust jackets with white lettering, and prices within one dollar of each other. The analogy with the automobile business seemed at times marvelously apt.

More important by far, however, is the fact that the competition has allowed—indeed forced—the best dictionaries to keep current as never before. Users who keep the newest college books at hand can have the most up-to-date information about the language available year after year and at modest cost. The good college books imitate each other slavishly on many points of format, encyclopedic information, and the like. *American Heritage II* has now adopted Merriam's separate alphabets for biographical, gazetteer, and other encyclopedic entries, rather than continue with the ACD-style single alphabet for all entries; I suspect that like Merriam, American Heritage finds the convenience and relatively lower cost of revisions of these smaller alphabets well worth whatever ease of use may be lost. It's only fair to point out, however, that in 1982, *American Heritage II* went to *blue* cloth binding and *blue* dust jacket in place of the ubiquitous red and gold bindings and red and white dust jackets! But the good dictionaries do differ in the details of lexicographic philosophy.

Editorially, the good college dictionaries clearly watch each other like hawks, and no one publishes a new edition without reading the competition's entries very carefully indeed. None would consider putting out a new edition that did not contain the latest census figures in its gazetteer entries, and most of the books will do their best to use these figures in the earliest reprinting for which they can be made available. This aspect of the competition simply underscores the importance of keeping current: the best books make certain that not only new words but new meanings, new pronunciations, and new statuses for words get picked up in any new edition and, where possible, in any new printing as well.

But there are still some very important differences in editorial policy and lexicographical style, and by working with all four of the current best dictionaries, and especially with the two most recent editions, *American Heritage II* and *Ninth Collegiate*, I've been able to get a pretty clear picture of current usage, current pronunciation, and the rest. It's thus the college dictionaries that have helped me most to sort out and evaluate not only some of the details of change in American English, but also some of the changes in attitude toward the language that have developed during that remarkable twenty-year stretch, 1966 to 1986.

CHAPTER 4

Vulgarity, Obscenity, and Lexicography

That college dictionaries and the American English they document had changed markedly over the last twenty years struck me almost from the moment I returned to the classroom. Two truisms, one about language and one about dictionaries, explain what I noticed first: (1) One of our most sensitive linguistic perceptions is the one that alerts us to the use of obscenities—the words Mother told us nice people didn't use—in unexpected places. (2) The first entries most male students look up in their new dictionaries are the four-letter words *fuck* and *shit*; that his new dictionary lacked entries for one or both of these words was the one fact that nearly every male in my freshman classes twenty years ago could have told me about his book, even if he had no idea of its date, publisher, or full title; twenty years ago, of course, it would never have occurred to me to poll the women in the class on that matter.

These truisms worked for me on my return, too. Among the first things I noticed were changes in the rules for use or suppression of obscene language. We notice these things right away, probably partly because we sense that to get them wrong can put us in serious trouble, and also partly—let's admit it—because we're curious. So it was with me.

Right away I noticed my students' much-increased use of obscene words and expressions in their talk among themselves, and sometimes even in their discussions with me and with other teachers. They used four-letter words much more frequently than I could remember having heard their parents use them twenty years ago in situations where the generations or the sexes were mixed. That observation led me to listen further afield, until I now conclude that not just students, but all sorts of people, including my peers and me, are now using many more of these words which prior to the mid-1960s would usually have been considered vulgar or

27

obscene; we're using them with greater frequency and also in a far wider variety of situations than would have been tolerated twenty years ago.

My first impression was that all the bars had been let down while I was away, and that the code of manners once controlling where and when the language's four-and-more-letter words of obscene and vulgar reference might safely be used had been completely revised. Expressions nearly everyone had considered obscene or vulgar and had therefore severely restricted in use just a couple of decades ago seemed now to have won tolerance, if not acceptance, in all sorts of new situations and in the mouths of all sorts of new speakers. The speech of the people around me—students and colleagues, friends and strangers alike—together with the newspapers, books, and magazines I read and the radio, motion pictures, theater, and television I heard and saw, all taught me that today I hear and see more of these formerly censored words, encountering them in environments and from speakers—women especially—in which and from whom they would almost never have been heard twenty years ago. And I note that even my own speech reflects this change: I am frequently surprised to hear some of my locker-room diction ring out in my own living room in my own voice and in mixed company.

In 1962, when Wilson Follett attacked *Webster III*, he thought its recognition of improved status for words whose use had hitherto been limited or taboo was part of a conspiracy by a "school" of linguists and lexicographers to lower or destroy all the standards of decency, tradition, and taste in language. There was of course no such "school," and even if there had been one, it could have been of no great effect because *all* the users of a language contribute to the setting of its standards, and, as we shall see in later chapters, we get the language we need and want and—perhaps—deserve. At any rate, as the Berkeley free speech movement spread to the nation's other campuses during the late 1960s, it was not just the appalled older generation that saw evidence everywhere suggesting that the bars were down. All sorts of people objected to the disreputable clothes and unkempt heads on view in public situations that had hitherto demanded jackets, ties, and grooming; all sorts too were unhappy about the language these ill-groomed, often ill-mannered "revolutionaries" frequently used. Some of the older generation were certain that standards of decency, tradition, and taste *were* under assault, and saw as one further bit of evidence the fact that youth worshipers among the middle-aged had begun to adopt youth's soiled beards, jeans, beads, sandals, and locutions almost more quickly than the unpliant young could set new modes. It seemed that obscenities and vulgarities, like grungy dress, had become shibboleths for being young and "part of the solution," rather than old and "part of the problem."

Gradually my observations led me to two questions: first, was the change in linguistic manners really as much of an about-face as it appeared to be, and second, was it as wide sweeping as it seemed: were *all* the bars coming down? To find out, I tested my impressions and tentative generalizations against the details reported in those most nearly current of all general dictionaries, the college books.

But first, just how expert are the college dictionaries as witnesses on these very sensitive matters, and second, what do they advise us? Among the hard questions for the editors and publishers of college dictionaries is whether to include in their books certain vulgar, obscene, or racially or ethnically derogatory words—words that have long had strong taboos attached to their general use. Most unabridged dictionaries, even though they must by definition be all-inclusive, have in fact only recently included entries for *fuck* and *shit*. For example, OED originally had an entry for *shit*, but didn't include *fuck*, which had been in English since at least the sixteenth century, until 1972, in volume 1 of its second supplement. *Webster III* (1961) has *shit*, but not *fuck*; *Webster II* (1934) had entries for neither. But for the makers and sellers of *college* dictionaries, the dilemma is much more difficult. Should the lexicographer and his publisher devote precious space in a dictionary, already necessarily much abridged under the constraints of size, cost, and the need to provide encyclopedic matter, to words that almost everyone considers "dirty"—vulgar, obscene, or in other ways offensive? In particular, should they record such words in commercial dictionaries aimed especially at a student market? A hard question, indeed.

In 1966 when I left teaching, in my judgment the four best college dictionaries on my desk were (alphabetically): *The American College Dictionary* (ACD), *The Standard College Diction-*

ary (SCD), *Webster's New World Dictionary of the American Language* (*New World*), and *Webster's Seventh New Collegiate Dictionary* (*Seventh New Collegiate*). In these four, published between 1958 and 1963, almost none of the "dirty" words or meanings could be found. Today's four best college dictionaries, however, reflect many differences—differences in the language, of course, but differences as well in manners and in the editorial policies that reflect them.

Deciding whether to include obscenities and vulgarities is by no means so easy for the lexicographer as it might at first appear, not least because any policy decision to exclude such words turns out to be nearly impossible to carry out in practice, given the way words change their meanings, functions, status, combined forms, and idiomatic uses. Lexicography is at least as much art as it is science. The polar answers to these questions are simple, but they conflict: on the one hand, even though many people object to "dirty" words, they *are* still part of the language; they exist, they are used, and hence it can be argued that any dictionary worthy of the name should include them. Moreover, many of these words have a high frequency of use, even if in limited situations; thus it can be argued that no abridged dictionary claiming to give an accurate picture of the most-used words in the vocabulary can omit them without distorting the accuracy of that picture.

On the other hand, these words are usually considered "bad" words, even by most of those who use them regularly. Wouldn't it be wiser to give them no further currency? By listing them in a book aimed at the student market in particular, is not the lexicographer naïvely warning the young not to put beans in their noses? Wouldn't it be wiser to omit such words entirely from this sort of book and leave to unabridged dictionaries (not so likely to be consulted by the young) the task of recording the whole language, warts and all? If the lexicographer includes such words, doesn't he risk teaching them to the young? One practical flaw in this latter argument appears at once: because lexicographers and their dictionaries do not create words, but merely report on those that already exist, it seems reasonable to assume that most dictionary users, young or old, will have encountered these high-frequency words elsewhere first; they will have to have heard or seen such words if they are to try to look them up. The counterargument urging the inclusion of such words therefore insists that the lexicographer give inquirers the information they seek concerning these words' precise meanings and peculiar statuses.

As I say, none of the four leading college dictionaries on my desk in 1966 had entries for the chief obscenities and vulgarities (but see footnote, p. 37). But in 1986, twenty years later, three of the four dictionaries that in my judgment are the current best contain almost all of these words and meanings. They are, alphabetically: *The American Heritage Dictionary*, second college edition (*American Heritage II*), *The Random House College Dictionary*, revised edition (*Random House Revised*), *Webster's New World Dictionary*, second college edition (*New World II*), and *Webster's Ninth New Collegiate Dictionary* (*Ninth New Collegiate*).

Since some of these vulgarities have been in the language for centuries, the decision to put them in college dictionaries now, after years of exclusion, appears to represent a major change in policy by the editors and publishers of these books. It may also suggest either that some of the words and their meanings have changed for the better over the past twenty years, or that society's attitudes toward them have undergone considerable modification, or, perhaps, both. Of course, it could simply be an editorial decision to be more candid, too.

In their front matter, neither *Random House Revised* nor *Ninth New Collegiate* discusses the problem of including vulgarities. Neither book describes the decision taken or the arguments that led to it; each simply includes these words and meanings and attaches such status labels as the editors deem accurate. *American Heritage II* states its position on the matter quite clearly by explaining three of the usage labels it employs for such words:

> *Vulgar.* The label Vulgar warns of social taboos attached to a word; the label may appear alone or in combination as *Vulgar Slang.*
>
> *Obscene.* A term that is considered to violate accepted standards of decency is labeled *Obscene.*
>
> *Offensive.* This label is reserved for terms such as racial slurs that are not only insulting and derogatory, but a discredit to the user as well. (49)

Examination of entries in all three dictionaries, however, shows that their editors all concluded that at least some vulgar words should be entered in the word list and accompanied by accurate descriptions of their meanings and their statuses (*Ninth New Collegiate*'s label is typically either "usu. considered obscene" or "usu. considered vulgar"). We can infer from the result only* that the editors took this decision in order to make their books more nearly accurate† and hence more useful. Although they didn't say so, possibly they also believed that accurate information about the meanings and especially about the status of these words would help all who inquire—including the young and unwary—to understand that these words are taboo on some or many levels and contexts of speech and writing, and that there is extremely strong animus in some quarters against their use, particularly among parental and other older generations (in the case of the "dirty" words of sex and defecation) and among the maligned groups themselves and their defenders (in the case of racially or ethnically derogatory terms).

The fourth of today's four leading college dictionaries, *New World II*, chose as a matter of policy *not* to include these vulgar words, although even having taken that decision, the editors couldn't avoid making some exceptions to it. In his foreword to *New World II*, Editor in Chief David R. Guralnik states both the problem and the policy decision he and his publishers made. Given the likelihood of its being favorably received by the righteous, perhaps Guralnik's candor isn't remarkable, but the absence of any direct discussion of these questions in the front matter of two of the other dictionaries suggests that their editors and publishers

---

*The location of *only* here gave me considerable pause when I was revising. My early drafts had it as I would speak it: "We can only infer," but subsequently I moved it to its present position immediately before the actual inference, the *that* clause. In speech we can put *only* almost where we will, logic or no, because our stress patterns will make its function clear. The contest between prose and speech causes no end of problems when editors prepare prose for publication. My own editor tells me that he would not have objected to *we can only infer.* My own reasoning was that the way I finally left it would not sound odd to anyone, whereas the other might possibly be noticed by a purist or two. I tried to please them all.

†Here's the much-argued question of whether some adjectives are simply incomparable (*unique, circular, pregnant*). *Useful,* I decided quite arbitrarily, was a state that could have degrees; some things could be more useful than others. But *accurate* seemed to me to be a specific state: either a report is accurate or it is not. (It could of course be *more nearly accurate than* another report, but neither would then be *accurate.*) One could argue over this, of course, and my judgment in this instance could be considered purist; I suspect, however, that few readers even noticed the distinction I drew between *useful* and *accurate,* although some conservatives might have disliked *more accurate.*

concluded that a discreet silence might be wiser than an open discussion of an editorial decision bound to rouse controversy once attention is called to it. *American Heritage II*'s editor and publishers handle the matter still differently: they list the three labels they use and describe succinctly what each means. (The approach *American Heritage II* takes is somewhat less direct than that taken by its first edition back in 1969, where the editor, William Morris, says flatly, "No word is omitted from the Dictionary merely because of taboo" [xlvi]. *American Heritage* did not then, nor does *American Heritage II* now, elaborate on the various aspects of the problem; nor does either book undertake to defend its position. Perhaps the editors of the second edition concluded that the first edition's statement was needlessly truculent, and that a somewhat less aggressive approach would be more prudent.)

But should we conclude from all this that *New World II* is smarmy or cowardly, that *Random House Revised* and *Ninth New Collegiate* are correct but timorous and hopeful only of avoiding confrontation on this issue, and that *American Heritage II* is the only one of today's good college dictionaries with courage? I think not. All four of these books are commercial ventures; to set out deliberately to anger potential customers is rarely the practice of skilled entrepreneurs, especially those who hope to continue in business. Guralnik's comments in his foreword to *New World II* remind us of the strong emotions vulgar language can evoke. When a practice such as putting "dirty" or "bad" words in a college dictionary is held by many to be morally indefensible, it's a fearless but probably imprudent businessman who takes the unpopular course and then publicly defends that action even before anyone has noticed and challenged it. I suspect that this commonsense point of view may account for the silence of the Merriam and Random House editors.

We can learn a good bit from Guralnik's remarks on this issue in his foreword to *New World II*, where in a brief paragraph he discusses two groups of vulgar words. Of the first group he says:

The absence from this dictionary of a handful of old, well-known vulgate terms for sexual and excretory organs and functions is not due to a lack of citations for these words from current literature. On the contrary, the profusion of such citations in recent years would suggest that the terms in question are so well known as to require no explanation. The decision to eliminate them as part of the extensive culling process that is the inevitable task of the lexicographer was made on the practical grounds that there is still objection in many quarters to the appearance of these terms in print and that to risk keeping this dictionary out of the hands of some students by introducing several terms that require little if any elucidation would be unwise. (viii)

This latter point is clear enough and fair enough: *New World II* concluded that to include vulgar words of this sort might adversely affect its sale in the school and college market. If it is to earn a profit for its producers, and if this dictionary, of which its editors are justifiably proud, is to reach the largest possible part of its intended audience, then the decision seems at least prudent. To include terms that many people do not want to see in print might cause parents, teachers, or school board members to consider the book unsuitable for the young. As many a recent public school library censorship battle has demonstrated, the world is full of people quite ready to use as a touchstone any word they consider vulgar or obscene; that is, for such people, simply to see the word is to have the measure of the book that contains it and to know that the book should be banned. The touchstone analogy is false, of course, but it is nonetheless a fact that its use is widespread, recurrent, and often effective. At any rate, given this possible penalty, *New World II*'s people decided that to include these vulgarities and obscenities was a gamble not worth taking.

But Guralnik's general statement can also mislead: he writes that "the profusion of . . . citations . . . would suggest that the terms in question are so well known as to require no explanation," but then says that such a conclusion was not the one that led to *New World II*'s decision to exclude certain vulgar terms. I accept this latter statement; the decision was almost certainly based on marketing concerns. But by having made that decision, *New World II*'s editors have in my opinion decreased the usefulness of their book. That this is so, I believe I can demonstrate by looking again at the first part of Guralnik's statement, and particularly by examining the implications of his comment about words "so well known as to require no explanation."

As a general principle for modern lexicography, that statement is wholly unacceptable, as Guralnik's following comment suggests. To pursue such a policy in treating the full vocabulary would be to destroy the utility of any general dictionary. Unfamiliar, low-frequency, "hard" words certainly need definition and other commentary, but so too do common, high-frequency words, perhaps especially because of their penchant for developing new, multiple meanings, their special susceptibility to functional and semantic change, and their resultant variation in status, particularly in their changed functions and transferred senses. In extremely high-frequency words, some senses, functions, and combined forms can develop a life of their own in a surprisingly short time. To imply that words "so well known as to require no explanation" need not be entered in the dictionary is to suggest (for example) that words such as *enter* and *come* or *screw* and *lay* need not be entered, and that not merely their primary or most common meanings but their functionally and semantically changed meanings and their combined forms* as well are all of such great familiarity as to require no comment. Not so. The principle is unsound, and of course *New World II* does not follow it in treating any of the vocabulary except when, by omitting certain vulgar words or the vulgar senses of certain words, it achieves the same effect. Were it to have followed the principle for the vocabulary as a whole, *New World II* would more nearly resemble some of the seventeenth-century ancestors of today's dictionaries, the so-called dictionaries of hard words, than it would modern college dictionaries. And *New World II* is in most respects a very good modern college dictionary.

Some of the most difficult-to-write and most detailed definitions any dictionary contains are those for some of the most common words in the language: nouns like *man* and *paper*, verbs like *shoot* and *start*, adjectives like *new* and *nice*, and the articles, prepositions, and auxiliaries. In 1962 the *Washington Post* editorially damned the then new unabridged *Webster III* for, among other sins, "pretentious and obscure verbosity" in its definition of "so simple an object as a door" (17 January 1962). *Webster III*'s definition of *door* begins:

---

*Functional change enables us to turn one part of speech into another: the verb *run* can become a noun, as in *to go for a run*, or to get one in a stocking. Semantic change is the development of a new meaning, as in *a home run* or in *Bull Run* (a stream). A combined form is a phrase whose semantic whole is different from the sum of its parts, as in *run off, run in, run out on, run through, run over, run up, run down*, and the like. (Consider *run up a bill* and *run down an acquaintance*—either in conversation or with a car.)

a movable piece of firm material or a structure supported usu. along one
side and swinging on pivots or hinges, sliding along a groove, rolling up
and down, revolving as one of four leaves, or folding like an accordion by
means of which an opening may be closed or kept open for passage into or
out of a building, room, or other covered enclosure or a car, airplane,
elevator, or other vehicle.

In a fine piece in *The Atlantic*, Bergen Evans responded by point-
ing out that the *Post*'s editorial writer "takes the plain, downright
man-in-the-street attitude that a door is a door and any damn fool
knows that." But, Evans continues,

> if so, he has walked into one of lexicography's biggest booby traps: the belief
> that the obvious is easy to define. Whereas the opposite is true. Anyone can
> give a fair description of the strange, the new, or the unique. It's the
> commonplace, the habitual, that challenges definition, for its very com-
> monness compels us to define it in uncommon terms. (59–60)

No, Guralnik has no intention of following a principle that most
common words (including vulgar ones) "require little if any elucidation" and "are so well known as to require no explanation."
But by omitting vulgarities for any reason, even for fear that some
people will refuse to buy books with bad words in them, *New World
II* omits some very high-frequency words for which there is a
"profusion of . . . citations in recent years." By so much does *New
World II* reduce its utility as a general college dictionary.

You see, with vulgar and obscene words there is a further
problem, however much the general public may believe that their
meanings are all too well known. Functional change, semantic
change, and the creation of new combined forms occur often with
astonishing rapidity in many of these words, and it's not just nuns,
other gentlewomen, or students reading American novels, plays,
and poems written before they were born who may be baffled by
such changes or curious about their status. Perhaps bafflement
comes about not least because of the strength of the taboos applied
to some of these words over the years; underground meanings are
hard to check.

But the main argument for including them in a dictionary is the
same as the argument for including as much of the entire vocabulary as possible: our age, our sex, our education, our associations
and isolations, and all the other limitations on our individual
experience mean inevitably that each of us on his own can grasp

only part of the elephant. Like the blind men in the fable, each of us has a different and limited personal experience of that elephant, language. It's the dictionary that can help those of us blinded by our personal provincialities to see the elephant whole.

Besides, *New World II*'s decision to eliminate some of these terms from the college dictionary is impossible to carry out completely anyway. There are "good" words that have developed "bad" meanings and "bad" statuses in those meanings. If a "good" word is entered in the dictionary, what is the editor to do about the "bad" meaning that exists whether he records it or not? Although *New World II* omits both the sense of *prick* meaning "penis" and its transferred meaning, "an obnoxious man or person," from its otherwise full treatment of the noun *prick*, in its entry for the verb *screw* it does record the meaning "to have sexual intercourse with" and gives it the label, *slang.* * The other three books label that sense "*Vulgar Slang*" (*American Heritage II*), "*Slang (vulgar)*" (*Random House Revised*), and "usu. considered vulgar" (*Ninth New Collegiate*). Then, further to the confusion of principle and practice, *New World II* records no definition of the noun *screw* meaning "an act of coitus"; *Random House Revised* has this meaning, and *American Heritage II* and *Ninth New Collegiate* record for the noun both that sense and "a partner in sexual intercourse."

New World II does record the transitive verb sense of *screw*, "to practice extortion on; cheat; swindle," and labels it "*Slang*," but does not give either the intransitive sense, "to engage in sexual intercourse," or its combined form, *to screw [someone] out of [something]*, which in one of its meanings could possibly be a transferred sense of the sexual meaning. Several slang uses— *screw up* as both noun and verb, for example, meaning "BOTCH, BLUNDER" (*Ninth New Collegiate*) or "1. a stupid mistake; blunder. 2. a habitual blunderer" (*Random House Revised*)—are recorded; *Ninth New Collegiate* attaches no label; *Random House Revised* labels these senses "*U.S. Slang*." Some of these transferred senses may derive from the vulgar senses; one or two indeed seem to

---

*Of all the vulgar or obscene words and senses I discuss in this chapter and the next, this sense of *screw*, "To copulate with," is the only one to be found in any of the four leading books that were on my desk in 1966. SCD (1963) included it and labeled it "Slang." The other three (ACD, *New World*, and *Seventh New Collegiate*) did not record that sense of the word, either as verb or noun.

me almost certainly to be slang euphemisms for *fuck* in the same
general senses and combinations. Compare, for example, *screwup*
and *fuckup* as nouns meaning both "a blunder" and "a blunderer,"
or the same two words as two-word combination verbs with similar
meanings: "to blunder (intransitive)" or "to break up or put out of
commission (transitive)." *American Heritage II, Random House
Revised,* and *Ninth New Collegiate* have several of these senses of
screw in its combined forms, and although the *Ninth* gives the verb
screw up no label at all, it is clear that the cluster of sexually derived
senses and the cluster of senses derived from the "good" meanings
of the word are becoming more and more closely intertwined and
inseparable. This means of course that some of the "dirt" may rub
off on the "clean" senses; but it also suggests that some of the "bad"
senses may be "improved" in some degree simply by their innocent
associations. Trends aren't yet wholly clear, but that's all the more
reason for a dictionary to give us as much information as possible.
The difference in impact that slang and vulgar slang can have on
one audience as compared with another can be prodigious, and the
young (who especially enjoy using slang) can unwittingly stumble
into worse than they know if their dictionaries will not light their
steps. Some coital senses of *screw* have already become slang and
are losing their vulgar status; some transferred senses are clearly
now and may indeed always have been only slang.

New World II's entry for *prick*, n., fails to explain some classmates' worldly laughter to the naïve youngster who, having stumbled into an unintentional double meaning, tries to find out what
happened and why. *American Heritage II* labels the "penis" sense
"*Vulgar Slang*." *Random House Revised* calls it "*Slang (vulgar),*"
and *Ninth New Collegiate* warns that it is "usu. considered vulgar." Nor does *New World II* help with the transferred sense of the
noun; but *American Heritage II* gives "A highly unpleasant person"
the "*Vulgar Slang*" label, *Random House Revised* labels "an obnoxious man; cad" "*Slang (vulgar),*" and *Ninth New Collegiate*
says that its sense of "A spiteful or contemptible person often
having some authority" is "usu. considered vulgar." Whether this
sense of the word will ever achieve a more elevated status cannot be
predicted. But it seems possible that for many, the old, literal sense
of "penis" will be more and more hidden by the much-used
figurative sense of "the obnoxious man." The fact is that the

transferred sense is much more widely used today—and in somewhat less-restricted circumstances—than was the case twenty years
ago. Some—especially the young—will need guidance, and the
dictionary ought to give it.

Nor is it just the young who may require the assistance *New
World II* fails to provide: an eighty-odd-year-old widow of my
acquaintance, an avid reader of modern plays, was a few years ago
baffled by a word she encountered in her reading. Suspicious that a
word like *prick* in its transferred senses as a noun was probably not
all it should be, she sought discreet help from her *New World*. No
luck. Even could she have overcome her reluctance to inquire
publicly, it's unlikely that many of the other elderly ladies in her
retirement home could have been very helpful. But most of today's
college books would have answered her question.

It's very clear, then, that the most recent lexicographic view is
that the "bad" words should be in the dictionary. The three most
recent editions of our four "best" books give them full entries and
labels. Most of those who make and sell college dictionaries have
done a full 180 degree turn on the subject of obscene words, and
this reversal has taken place within the last twenty years. It's a full
change in policy, and taken together with some of the other
changes we'll see in the way contemporary American society looks
at obscenities and vulgarities, it can startle any Van Winkle.

In the next chapter, we'll look at some details of Taboo No. 1,
and then examine some further implications of this major change
in the manners of American English.

CHAPTER 5

Bad Words: The Gelding of Taboo No. 1

This chapter could be uncomfortable going for some readers, and others could find the explicit documentation of several four-letter words downright distressing. I don't detail these matters lightly; to document what I conclude is a very significant change in linguistic manners, I've felt obliged to present information from the dictionaries' entries on words that, although everyone knows they exist, not everyone sees any need to explore. But I present these matters with no sophomoric intent to titillate or shock. The plain truth is that when I returned, the very first big change I saw in the language and in our attitudes toward it was the unraveling of the once-powerful taboo against the use of certain sexual and excretory obscenities. Together with the change I discuss in chapter 6, I think it makes one of the key points of this book.

Some uses of two of the most reprehended but most widely used vulgar obscenities, *shit* and *fuck*, have changed enough in both meaning and status that most of today's college dictionaries report in full on them, even though for most ears and eyes nearly all uses remain below normal standards of propriety for speech and writing. Neither of these words—both of them very old in English—was in any of the four leading college dictionaries in 1966; three of today's four leaders report them.

The reasons they ought be reported are, first, that we hear them more and more these days, on the stage and at the movies, in factories and offices where men and women work together, in the school yard and on the campus, in the tavern and at the cocktail party. We ought to be as sensitive to changes in their use as we are to changes in the other manners of our time, both in the unpliant young and in those of their elders who insist on imitating them. And second, we need to have reports because we see these words more and more often in print (as Guralnik observed in his foreword to *New World II*), both in the literary representation of our conversation and in the journalism that reports the facts of contemporary behavior. *Shit* may indeed be ordure and therefore fundamentally unacceptable in any polite use, but today the word has more than one transferred sense with wholly different and—at least to some people in some circumstances—less abhorrent referents. There are a few combined forms of it that seem to me to be widely (albeit sometimes nervously) accepted in conversation within all but the most formal or conservative constituencies.

The recent history of the word *shit* suggests that its excremental/excretory meanings as noun and verb (and in a combined form such as *shithouse*, which at least in some uses retains the vulgar literal meaning) are not the meanings most frequently encountered by present-day hearers and readers of Standard English or anything approaching it.

New World II of course does not have an entry for the word, but a good deal of information about linguistic change and variation shows up in a review of what the other three of today's best college dictionaries report about the word.

Random House Revised reports the doubled *t* of the *-ing* spelling; *American Heritage II* gives us that plus a variant strong verb preterit, * *shat*, and a regular *-s* form (for third-person singular verb or noun plural). *Ninth New Collegiate* gives separate entries for verb and noun, notes that both were probably in English before the twelfth century, and reports both the *-ing* and strong preterit verb forms. *Random House Revised* also notes the word's use as an interjection. *American Heritage II* and *Ninth New Collegiate* report both transitive and intransitive literal senses of the verb: "to defecate," and "to defecate in." All three books record essentially the same meanings for the noun: (1) "excrement or feces," (2) "the act of defecation," and (3) "foolishness, nonsense" (*Ninth New Collegiate* and *American Heritage II*), and "pretense, exaggeration, lies, or nonsense" (*Random House Revised*). All these meanings are labeled: *American Heritage II* calls them all "*Obscene*," *Ninth New Collegiate*, "usu. considered vulgar," and *Random House*

Preterit is just another name for the past tense form in verbs. *Strong* verbs change the vowel for past tense: *swim-swam*; *weak* verbs add the so-called dental suffix to form the preterit: *try-tried*.

Revised, "Slang (vulgar)." Philologists might remind us that in its literal senses the word was probably standard even as late as Chaucer's and Langland's time. But statuses change; today not every cheerful fellow wants to be called *gay*. In any event, it's clear that the taboos of vulgarity and obscenity have long lain heavily on the word in its literal senses and functions.

Nonetheless, today there are some curious points to be considered, one involving *American Heritage*, which in its 1969 first edition gave another transitive sense for the verb, "to deceive or mislead," as in *You wouldn't shit me, would you?* which it labeled *"Vulgar Slang,"* although it labeled the literal sense of the verb simply *"Vulgar."* But *American Heritage II* (1982) drops both this figurative sense and the distinction in labels; in my judgment, this sense today is at least as widely used as one of the noun senses *American Heritage II* retains ("foolishness"). The earlier edition also reports several noun meanings, all marked *"Vulgar Slang"*; two of these have disappeared from the 1982 edition: "a narcotic drug; especially, heroin," and "a highly objectionable person." *Ninth New Collegiate* records the drug definition, but not the still very common vulgar slang appellation for a person much disliked.

One might conclude from this brief review that *American Heritage II*'s editors had decided to be less detailed and so make less of a thing of these words than their predecessors had done in the earlier edition. Perhaps that's what happened. In my opinion, however, on most counts *American Heritage*'s earlier treatment of the word provided a more nearly accurate account of the word's use and status both then and now than does *American Heritage II*'s more limited 1982 coverage. At any rate, it seems to me that in the figurative, nonfecal senses of noun, verb, and interjection, the taboo on *shit* today is considerably less stringent in some situations and for some speakers and perhaps for some writers than it was in the early 1960s, and probably a good deal less stringent even than it was when *American Heritage* first appeared in 1969.

The frequency with which today we encounter the transferred senses of *shit* as verb and noun, "to deceive or mislead" and "nonsense," or "an objectionable person," suggests that although anathematized in most polite use, some meanings and functions of the word have begun to change status a bit, even though because of their older, primary meanings they are not likely to reach full acceptance in our time, or perhaps ever. But I hear mixed groups of college students and occasionally of older adults as well use these two terms with great frequency, and I consider some of the groups from which I've heard them to be otherwise unexceptionable in manners and other signs of conventional deportment. Something has changed.

Other curious points appear when we examine some functionally changed and compounded forms of the word; these continue to develop. Surprisingly, only one of our four present-day college dictionaries records the widely heard adjective *shitty*; its referent is almost never ordure: "1. inferior or contemptible. 2. inept or insignificant" are *Random House Revised*'s definitions, where the entire entry carries the label *"Slang (vulgar)." American Heritage II* reports a compound, *shithead*, which it labels *"Vulgar Slang,"* and defines as "a highly contemptible or objectionable person," almost the precise definition the 1969 *American Heritage* gave for one figurative sense of the noun *shit*.

Random House Revised also reports the compound noun *shit list* (which I have also seen hyphenated and as a single word). It means "a list of people strongly disliked or in great disfavor," as nearly everyone today between the ages of sixteen and sixty must surely know. None of the other three current dictionaries records it, but even more important, *Random House Revised* labels it merely "U.S. Slang," not *vulgar* or *obscene* or otherwise taboo. Certainly there are many situations in which its use will still cause eyebrows, hackles, or even gorges to rise, particularly among older people, but there are large and growing parts of the population now regularly accustomed to hearing or speaking if not reading or writing the word, and most of these people would be hard-pressed to find a synonym. It seems to me that we must conclude that *shit list* is no longer obscene; it has achieved at least a modicum of acceptability as American slang. In the 1960s none of the leading college dictionaries mentioned the term, although it was almost certainly in wide but not accepted use then. Clearly its status has undergone considerable amelioration in the last twenty years.

Another interesting compound with a changing status is *bull-shit*, a word we regularly encounter as noun, verb, and interjection, and occasionally as noun adjunct or adjective, too. But it's always used in a figurative sense. *Ninth New Collegiate* and *Ran-*

dom House Revised both record the word; *New World II* and *American Heritage II* do not. *American Heritage* (1969) had a full entry for *bullshit*, defining the noun as "Foolish, uninformed, or exaggerated talk," and the intransitive verb as "To utter such talk." It labeled both functions "*Vulgar Slang.*" One can only speculate on why *American Heritage II* dropped the term, but it does retain an entry for the probably euphemistic clipped form, *bull* (as in *He talks a lot of bull* or *He bulled his way through the exam*). The other three current books also have entries for the clipped euphemism— if, indeed, that's what this form of *bull* really is.

The etymologies for these senses of *bull* show variety and imagination: *Random House Revised* proposes "[<*bulla* play, game, jest (whence also Icel *bull* nonsense)]," while *Ninth New Collegiate* lists at least two: for "a grotesque blunder in language," "*n* [per. fr. obs. *bull* to mock]," and for [6]*bull*, meaning "to engage in idle and often boastful talk" and "to fool esp. by fast boastful talk," as well as for the related noun meaning "empty boastful talk" and "NONSENSE," "[short for *bullshit*]." *New World II*'s entry for *bull*[3] offers "[ME. *bul*, trickery, lie < OFr. *boule*, lie < L. *bulla*: see prec.]"; but when we look at the preceding, we find *New World II* coming boldly out of the closet to explain one euphemism with another: for the noun *bull*[1] 7., we get "[clip of *bull* "dung" (a euphemism)] [Slang] foolish, insincere, exaggerated, or boastful talk; nonsense." It's another illustration of the silly contortions to which the policy of trying to exclude "bad" words can lead a lexicographer. What we really do need to notice is that all these uses of *bull* as euphemisms for *bullshit* are labeled *slang* and nothing worse; all such senses are figurative, not literal.

Perhaps one other difference among the various treatments of the word *shit* and its derivatives deserves comment. As I point out above, only *Random House Revised* cites the word's use as an interjection; yet surely this is one of its most common uses.

The word *fuck* illustrates even more fully some of the kinds of functional change often typical of this sort of vulgar word (compare *piss*, *pissed off* "angry," and *pissed* "angry or drunk," for example), as well as the semantic changes through which transferred senses of the word can come to considerable currency in the speech and even in the writing of those who would rarely or never use the word in any of its primary or literal senses. Above all, *fuck* displays

considerable development of combined forms, with words such as
up, *off*, and *with*, each with a different idiomatic meaning having
nothing to do with coitus. The current college dictionaries define
several of these, whereas twenty years ago, none of the four best
college books even had an entry for the base word itself.

American Heritage II has five related entries, and it labels all
these senses, functions, and forms *"Obscene"* (its 1969 edition
drew distinctions between the *"Vulgar"* label for literal senses and
"Vulgar Slang" for figurative ones, but that distinction has disappeared from the 1982 edition). *Random House Revised* has two
main entries and labels both in all senses *"Slang (usually) vulgar)"*;
the labels make no distinction between the literal and figurative
senses. *Ninth New Collegiate*, however, in its three entries, does
draw distinctions with its labels: essentially, regardless of function,
the literal senses are "usu. considered obscene," and the figurative
senses are "usu. considered vulgar."

All three books record the transitive and intransitive verbs meaning "to copulate" and "to copulate with." *American Heritage II* also
lists the following as "phrasal verbs": *"fuck around.* To fool around.
fuck off. To leave at once. *fuck over.* To treat unfairly; take advantage of. *fuck up* 1. To bungle. 2. To act carelessly or foolishly."

Random House Revised lists two figurative transitive verb senses:
"2. to treat unfairly or harshly. 3. to bungle or botch (usually fol.
by *up*)" and a figurative intransitive sense, "5. to meddle (usually
fol. by *with*)." *Ninth New Collegiate* lists the same figurative
intransitive sense as does *Random House Revised*: "2: MESS—used
with *with*"; it also has a transitive sense, "2: to deal with unfairly or
harshly: CHEAT, DO IN."

The participial *-ing* form of the verb gets a separate entry in
Random House Revised, defined as "damned" for both adjectival
and adverbial uses. In its verb entry, *Ninth New Collegiate* reports
that *fuck* is "sometimes used in the present participle as a meaningless intensive." Its noun entry also records a use "with *the* as a
meaningless intensive; usu. considered vulgar ⟨ what the ~ do they
want from me?⟩." *Random House Revised* covers the "damn" sense
in its definition of the word used as an interjection: "damn (used as
an expletive, often fol. by *you*)."

Other combined forms occur: *American Heritage II* also has
separate entries for *fucked-up* ("Totally confused, mismanaged, or

disordered") and the noun *fuckup* ("1. One who fucks up. 2. A blunder; bungle."). *Ninth New Collegiate* covers both these functions in a single entry: "*vi* . . . : to act foolishly or stupidly: BLUNDER . . . *vt*: to ruin or spoil esp. through stupidity, ignorance, or carelessness: BUNGLE . . . *fuckup* . . . *n.*"

Random House Revised and *Ninth New Collegiate* both record the noun *fucker* without definition as a run-on at the end of their verb entries; *American Heritage II* gives *fucker* a separate entry, defined "1. One that fucks. 2. One that is offensive." My own opinion is that the term requires its own definition, although I would prefer something a bit more specific than *American Heritage II's* second sense. It's my observation that the word is rarely used in the literal sense suggested by the agentive *-er* suffix; rather, I hear it used mainly as a contemptuous, derogatory, or otherwise opprobrious term of near-expletive strength and use, applied to a person or thing (such as a man deserving scorn or anger, or an engine that won't start). It's both vulgar and slang in that use, I believe, but not obscene.

One final curiosity: none of the three dictionaries that record the word cites the combined form *fuck off* as an intransitive verb meaning "to evade or fail to perform tasks or duties," or as a noun (usually spelled *fuck-off* or *fuckoff*) meaning "a person who evades duty or fails to perform, a slacker." *American Heritage II* has the "phrasal verb" *fuck off*, but only with the meaning "To leave at once." All these missing "goof-off" senses, in both functions, had very wide currency as vulgar slang after World War II (where they seem to have begun with the military), but all of them can still be heard occasionally today in certain mixed groups of the young, and in the sixtyish male population. The latter group seem generally to continue to restrict the use of the terms to the kind of predominantly male groups in which they first learned to use them in their military youth. The current college dictionaries may have assessed accurately the fading of these meanings and so decided not to include them, but it's my guess that teachers of the literature of the twentieth century may regret the omission.

At any rate, change and some small amelioration appear to have occurred in the figurative senses of this word and its combinations; their frequency of use since the 1960s or perhaps a bit earlier has become greater and has appeared in a widening variety of constituencies and situations, in both the written and spoken language. All remain "dirty" words, often used for their power to shock by the young and their imitators, but the words live in these mainly oral slang uses almost exclusively in their figurative senses, at least among speakers of Standard or near-Standard English. Recently, as a group of university students straggled from a final examination in the classroom across the hall from my office, I saw and heard one attractively dressed young woman observe to the others in the mixed group, "God, he really fucked us on that second question!" Neither she nor her friends male or female appeared to me to be noticeably abandoned, immoral, or in other respects vulgar.

It seems clear from the lexicographical and anecdotal evidence I've examined that the transferred senses and combined forms of the word *fuck* are appearing today in social contexts very different from those to which we might have expected to see and hear them limited a couple of decades ago. One might well argue that vulgar is vulgar and that that is all one needs to know, but anyone interested in the changing manners of our society should not ignore this linguistic development. Substantial numbers of today's student generation have begun using these words, in transferred senses and combined forms at least, to such an extent that we must conclude that many of them consider these words fairly or even wholly acceptable for communication with most of their peers, even in sexually mixed groups. And so too, I think, do those of their elders who imitate their children and their students in dress and other manners, including language.

Probably this change is not attributable only to the young and their imitators, or at least not to the current crops alone. We need to remind ourselves that today's college students were barely in rompers when the free speech movement left Berkeley in the late 1960s and began to spread across the country. And in the decade that followed, a generation of exceedingly outspoken youth determined to shed or pretend to shed its inhibitions both sexual and linguistic and to free itself of repressions of almost every kind. It shouldn't surprise us now, therefore, that today's language reflects some of this social change, even if some of that generation have today turned into rather conventional yuppies.

But what difference does it make? *Fuck* is a "bad" word, isn't it? What has *New World II* lost by failing to record it at all? What have the other three dictionaries lost by omitting one or another of the figurative, compounded, or functionally changed senses of the word? And what have *American Heritage II* and *Random House Revised* lost by not distinguishing between the obscene and the vulgar or vulgar slang uses of some of these words and senses? One loss, it seems to me, occurs when a college dictionary fails to use its greatest strength, its currency. And if the college dictionaries don't keep us informed, we—the users of dictionaries—stand to lose the most.

We know further that in the informal parts of the vocabulary, and especially in the slang, changes of this sort can occur very quickly indeed. Older generations may well wish that such changes would not occur, but wishing won't make it so, as the whole history of the English lexicon makes clear. In the end, we can enforce our views only on ourselves and perhaps on our children while they are still very young and pliant. (But one of my colleagues observes, "I'm stunned when I hear seven-year-olds casually say, 'Spinach sucks.'" Perhaps the innocents still hit hardest of all.) The differences in linguistic standards between the generations are only now being truly appreciated for their great power and influence. *American Heritage*'s distinguished but elderly usage panel and this year's newly initiated Phi Beta Kappas would almost certainly differ over a good many usage items, vulgarities and obscenities among them. Perhaps only social class has as much effect on linguistic judgments of usage as differences in ages of speakers and listeners have. We'll look further at this matter in chapter 9, but first there's a bit more to be said about the gelding of Taboo No. 1.

The seasoned old swear words, *damn* and *god-damned* (in several spellings and pronunciations), and the words *God* and *hell* as expletives, interjections, or just plain cusswords, although not always vulgar (they do, after all, live very respectable lives in biblical English), have had various taboos and restrictions placed on them almost from the beginning. "Taking the name of the Lord in vain" has been strongly prohibited in many parts of society, although it is difficult to assess the numbers of people who rigorously enforce that taboo today, either because of religious scruple or just for good manners. In 1966 only *New World* noted the use of *God* as an exclamation. None of the 1966 books had an entry for *god-awful*, and only two—*SCD*, which had a full discussion of the various ways *god-damned* was being used, and *New World*, which described *god-damned* as "a curse or strong intensive"—listed that ubiquitous and variously spelled compound.

Today, in their entries for *God*, only *Random House Revised* and *New World II* cite the word's use as an interjection. *God-awful*, either run together or hyphenated, is labeled "*Slang*" by *American Heritage II*, "*Informal*" by *Random House Revised*, and carries no label at all in *Ninth New Collegiate*.

Even in 1966 the labels for *damn* and *damned*, for which all four leading college dictionaries had entries, were not strongly restrictive: *ACD* said the two forms were used in swearing or for emphasis, and labeled both "[Colloq.]"; *SCD* called most swearing uses "*Informal*"; *Seventh New Collegiate* identified *damn* as a "curse" and an interjection, and labeled it "*colloq.*" Today all four of the leading college dictionaries give a very full treatment to *damn* in all its spellings, all its functional shifts (as adjective, adverb, interjection, etc.), and all its combinations, with the only labels occurring on any sense of the word being *informal* or *colloquial*. Clearly, our attitudes toward this word, and toward *hell* as a cussword as well, have become more and more tolerant as the word in these senses has spread through wider and more general use by more and more of the population. The taboos that used to control in polite society continue to weaken. *Damn* and *hell* are simply not very powerful words these days. And who can be certain that none of the other "bad" words we have been discussing will go the same route one day? It's been just forty-seven years since Clark Gable pioneered *damn* as a noun in the motion picture version of *Gone with the Wind*—not a long time. But the trend seems unchanged.

Some of my generation may well wonder as they listen to the college students in today's halls whether these youngsters are an unusually depraved and degraded generation. In my judgment they are nothing of the sort; the observation to be made is rather that manners—and the language is part of manners—are changing. The language and other manners of the flapper generation of the 1920s fared no better with its elders, I'm told. On balance, with manners changing (at least in the entrenched elder generation's view) always for the worse, we ought not be surprised to discover that the young appear to be leading the way in many of what seem to us the more disturbing aspects of linguistic change. *Fuck* and *shit* illustrate the point well. My generation of World War II servicemen actually developed and refined much of the functional change and most of the transferred senses and combined forms of these words, but we restricted their use—together with use of the older, primary senses of these words—almost exclusively to the barracks, the field, and the tavern. When we came home, for the most part we continued to restrict them to the male bastions— the workplace and the locker room. We gave the words increasingly widespread currency (with euphemisms where needed: consider *snafu*—"situation normal, all *fouled* up"—and all its cousins), but in rigorously limited, generally male-only situations where vulgar slang was accepted and, indeed, expected. In the past twenty years we have seen the young spread these words and senses into other, wider social situations. We may well be shocked, but we ought not be surprised. Some of my generation, then in their undecided middle age, adopted these changes in linguistic manners, in imi- tation or in pursuit of youth, just as some of them also aped the jeans and beards which the 1960s and 1970s generation of the young made so popular.

That some segments of American society—especially the young—have managed to bring some vulgar language out of the barracks, the pool hall, and the factory and let some bits of it (functionally and semantically changed, oftentimes) ring in nearly everyone's ears, is something we cannot ignore. No doubt maga- zines, books, the movies, and the theater have helped, and uncen- sored cable television and video cassettes promise to help even more. But it hasn't been just the young who have paid to see these productions and hear their language. Further, I have no doubt that the new attitudes of women have had considerable effect on the disappearance of some of the old taboo: many women, mainly but not exclusively the outspoken young, have deliberately adopted language hitherto restricted to males, just as they have attacked other social taboos once applied only to women. You've come a long way linguistically, too, Baby! But the main thing is the change itself. The taboo has been gelded.

Whether we want to fight it, join it, or simply wring our hands over it, we need to be aware of the nature and the extent of this change in manners. Our observations may lead to different conclu- sions: the change may be a sign of freedom from inhibition and repression; or it may indicate that indeed standards are sliding and that the Moral Majority is right about where we are headed. But I doubt it. Every sign I see suggests that these changes in language, like the Renaissance's adoption of "inkhorn" terms (typically, polysyllabic Latin words, such as *aureate* for *golden*), simply reflect the changing of manners over time. Nineteenth- and twentieth-century bourgeois churchgoers and taxpayers made the same sort of thing happen (and are still doing it) when repeatedly they appropriated the argot of the underworld—words such as *tail* for "follow," *dip* for "pickpocket," and *john* for the prostitute's prospective customer. These changes too simply remind us that manners change as time passes. Other changes bother some of us even more, as when "a perfectly good word" such as the adjective *gay* moves as it has in the past twenty years or so from also carrying a cant meaning, "homosexual," to a point today where that meaning, both as adjective and noun, has overwhelmed or tainted all older senses of the word. No wonder many writers and speakers now avoid the word in the older meanings entirely.

But the changes in the old "dirty" or "bad" words are the main issue here. We can tinker with these slang changes in the language (we will seldom have much effect one way or the other on the older, primary senses); we can occasionally block or slow some of the transferred senses in a few small particulars, or we may be able to foster and hurry some of them along by adopting them in our own speech and prose (e.g., *shit list*); but in the final analysis, the important thing and the humanist's duty are to observe these changes accurately and try to understand what they mean both in themselves and as signs of larger patterns of changing values in this society.

Rip Van Winkle was shocked to discover that describing himself as "a loyal subject of King George" was no longer the thing at all. On my return to the study of the language, I was surprised at the extent of the change in the currency and status of some meanings and forms of words that, when I fell asleep to them, were clearly and nearly always considered obscene or vulgar or both and were strictly limited in use. Lexicographers have reflected this change today by including these terms in their college dictionaries. The unabridged *Random House Dictionary of the English Language*, first published in 1966, had no entries for *shit* and *fuck*, perhaps in part because the much-maligned 1961 *Webster III did* enter one of them. Nor did *ACD*, Random House's older and excellent college dictionary (it was still in print in 1966), nor did any of the other three leading college dictionaries of that year contain either of these words. Yet both had been in the language for centuries. But today's Random House college book, *Random House Revised*, one of the four best now available, enters both words and treats them both fully. So too do two of today's other fine books. That remarkable change has taken less than twenty years.

CHAPTER 6

Worse Words: The Power of Taboo No. 2

So much for Taboo No. 1, against the vulgar words of sex and excretion and the well-worn words of swearing. What then of the second great taboo, concerning that other class of "bad" words that *New World II* decided to exclude, the racially and ethnically derogatory terms? Guralnik's foreword to *New World II* continues: "In a similar vein, it was decided in the selection process that this dictionary could easily dispense with those true obscenities, the terms of racial or ethnic opprobrium, that are, in any case, encountered with diminishing frequency these days" (viii). The rhetorical impact of the word *true*—"those *true* obscenities"—is doubled-edged: it reveals on the one hand the fact that the taboo on racial and ethnic slur language is extremely strong today, and it invites us on the other hand to infer that the sexual and excretory language that *New World II* also excluded might not really be obscene after all, at least by comparison!

If by "in a similar vein" Guralnik means again "for marketing reasons," then *New World II's* exclusion of terms such as *nigger*, *kike*, *ofay*, *hunky*, and *honky* is clearly practical; in this instance, however, a far larger portion of the population doesn't like them, won't use them, and wants them to disappear, than is the case with words such as *fuck* and *shit*. But "in a similar vein" presumably does not include the "so well known as to require no explanation" comment Guralnik made on the other class of vulgarities and obscenities. Here, indeed, his argument is that this class of racial and ethnic words is being "encountered with diminishing frequency these days." But again, what are dictionaries for—especially college dictionaries? Practical considerations include the needs of those whose college dictionaries ought to help them read the literature of the recent past. *Sheeny* and *honky* both occur in much-read fiction of the past forty years, for example, as well as in the drama; until annotated editions of the literature appear, a dictionary is the most likely source for the reader's guidance. But if these words are not likely to be encountered except in annotated literature of considerable age, if Dos Passos and Steinbeck now come with glossaries for students, then these words indeed have little claim on space in a crowded abridgment that is concentrating on today's language.

Again with the racial and ethnic terms as with the sexual and excretory ones, Guralnik's position is unassailable by the righteous. And in this case, unlike that of the other group of vulgar words, a large and growing part of society is consciously censoring the use of such terms, even in informal or jocular use. Among some groups, racial and ethnic epithets have been made obsolete since the mid-1960s by means of one of the strongest and most effective taboos I've ever seen, a taboo rigorously enforced among social liberals of all kinds, and among social conservatives with good manners. The taboo is not yet effective for the whole society; Archie Bunker still lives, but he's surrounded, and, as we shall see, that part of his vocabulary is being driven underground.

Diminishing frequency of occurrence is a good reason for excluding words from an abridged dictionary; that's why most college dictionaries began dropping certain older Scottish dialect words that today's American reader encounters almost solely in the novels of Walter Scott or the poetry of Robert Burns. But with terms such as *bohunk* or *ofay*, I submit that the situation is different on two counts. Burns died in 1796, Scott in 1832. Their literary use of Scots dialect words is now more than 150 years old. *Wop* and *spi(c)(k)*, however, appear in American literature of this century, especially in work published since 1920. Furthermore, these terms, although they now show signs of obsolescence even where they are not wholly taboo, are still in use among certain segments of the population, especially among the entrenched elderly in the lower parts of the social, economic, and educational scales and in certain ill-mannered, reactionary parts of the society at all social class levels. We therefore require a different sort of judgment to help decide whether to put these words in a college dictionary. Clearly, all of them need not be reported, especially those we now encounter only in literature written long ago and seldom read today except in school where text or teacher can annotate. But some others still warrant entry, however offensive we may deem them; not least among the reasons for entering them in these books is that we may thus guide the young and the inexperienced not only as to the meanings of words wholly unfamiliar to them, but also as to the increasingly important strengths of the taboo involved. And there are traps for the unwary that can only consciously be learned: only the more sensitive Scots in this country object to the term *Scotchman* (preferring *Scot* or *Scotsman*), although some may at least judge the user ignorant; but for *Chinaman*, which at a glance looks to be made of similarly harmless stuff, *Ninth New Collegiate* still feels obliged (correctly, I believe) to guide the inexperienced with a label: "often taken to be offensive." *American Heritage II* and *Random House Revised* also warn that the term will offend.* But the entry for *Chinaman* in *New World II* (despite the editors' decision not to include such words) clinches the point: "now generally regarded as a contemptuous or patronizing term." When *Irishman* and *Frenchman* pose no problem, American youngsters can scarcely be expected to guess on their own that *Chinaman* may be objectionable; they need advice.

There are interesting differences between the way the four best college dictionaries of 1966 handled these words and the way the four best treat them today.

Nigger appeared in all four books in 1966; all gave two senses, "Negro," and "any dark-skinned person," and all four entries were assigned the strongest sort of restrictive label: *ACD*: "offensive"; *SCD*: "a vulgar and offensive term"; *Seventh New Collegiate*: "usu. taken to be offensive"; and *New World*: "A vulgar and offensive term of hostility and contempt, used by Negrophobes." Today, *New World II* no longer enters the word at all, under the policy I've described above, but the other three of today's leaders do, in both senses, and with strongly restrictive labels.

Ofay (pig Latin for *foe*?) is a term apparently of relatively recent origin (*Ninth New Collegiate* gives 1917 as its earliest printed

---

*My colleague Thomas Roberts comments: "I have read somewhere that the angry young Chinese Americans who are fighting racism insist upon the word *Chinamen* now. I suppose we could have predicted that they would reject liberal pieties and choose a word that had a slightly pejorative halo to resurrect as a banner." None of the college dictionaries reports this change, nor do William and Mary Morris in their 1985 *Harper Dictionary of Contemporary Usage*, 2d ed. But changes of this sort can rise (and fall) almost overnight.

appearance). In 1966 only *SCD* ("*U.S. Slang* a white man") and *Seventh New Collegiate* ("*Slang* a white person") listed the word. Today, three of the four leaders enter it and assign labels stronger than the "Slang" labels of 1966: *American Heritage II*: "*Offensive Slang.*" *Random House Revised*: "Disparaging." *Ninth New Collegiate*: "usu. used disparagingly."

On the face of it, the pattern for the term *honky* in its various spellings seems to be the same: in 1966 none of the four leading books listed the word, but today three of the four leaders have it. *Ninth New Collegiate* reports the earliest citation of the word to be 1967, after the four 1966 leaders were published. The word may well have been in oral use indefinitely earlier, but we would not normally expect college dictionaries to pick up the word without some firm, usually printed, documentation. Today *American Heritage II* labels this term, which it defines as "A white person," as "*Offensive Slang.*" *Random House Revised* labels it "Disparaging" and says it is "used esp. by blacks." *Ninth New Collegiate* notes "usu. used disparagingly." *New World II* has no entry for *honky*.

It's clear that terms of racial and ethnic derogation are frowned on today whether they're applied to the minority or to the majority. The majority apparently was not troubled by *ofay* in 1966, and the *slang* label was enough, but today it's "disparaging" and "offensive." Sensibilities have become much more tender over the past twenty years, and not just minority sensibilities, either. It is also clear that *ofay* and *honky* appear frequently in the work of recent black American authors, but most of these writers have not yet been published in annotated editions; many readers—and not just the young—will need help with both the meaning and the status of these terms. They belong in college dictionaries today.

Several dated terms of racial or ethnic derogation reflect a similar pattern of increased editorial attention or at least stronger opinions on the status of such words over the years since 1966. *Kike*, "A Jew," appeared in two of the 1966 books: *SCD* labeled it "*Slang* . . . a vulgar and offensive term*"; *New World* said it was "[Slang] . . . vulgar, offensive term of hostility and contempt, as used by anti-Semites." Neither *ACD* nor *Seventh New Collegiate* listed it. Today again only two of the four leading college dictionaries have the word: *Random House Revised* labels it "Offensive," and *Ninth New Collegiate* says it is "usu. taken to be offensive."

New World II of course does not contain the word, following its general editorial principle discussed above. *American Heritage II* also omits the word, but for what I believe is a different reason. The earlier (1981) "New College Edition" of *Heritage* did have the word *kike*, which it labeled "*Slang . . .* An offensive term used derogatorily." I judge, therefore, that the word was dropped from the latest edition, *American Heritage II*, because the editors believed that its current frequency of use was so low as to class it with some of Scott's dialect words rather than with present-day English, at least in the hard-fought contest for the limited space a college dictionary has to devote to archaic or obsolete words. And if, indeed, this means that the word is less frequently encountered now than even in 1981, then here we can see a good illustration of the effectiveness of the recently reinforced taboo against such terms of ethnic derogation, not an editorial decision, but society's.

Sheeny, another anti-Semitic epithet, appeared in that sense in none of the 1966 books, apparently on the unspoken but then widely held belief that neither words like this nor the sexual and excretory terms need be or *should* be in college dictionaries. Today, however, the anti-Semitic *sheeny* appears in two of the four leaders, which label it "*Offensive Slang*" (*American Heritage II*) and "*Offensive*" (*Random House Revised*). *Ninth New Collegiate* does not have it, but since it omits the word when its parent unabridged, *Webster III*, has it and marks it "usu. taken to be offensive," I conclude that the editors judged this word too to be dying out. I agree: I can read the word in American books written earlier in this century, but I haven't heard the word used more than twice in the last fifteen years, I think, both times by the same elderly rural laborer. In 1966 the word existed but probably could reasonably have been labeled *archaic*; it was clearly on the way to becoming obsolete. Today it has all the currency of *twenty-three skidoo*, a fact reflected in the judgment of at least one dictionary's editorial staff, which while perfectly willing to print and label racial and ethnic terms of derogation, was unwilling to waste space in an abridged book of this sort on dead or dying words. In another decade, if the taboo holds, *sheeny* and some others like it might very well and very reasonably be dropped from all the college dictionaries.

Wop, a derogatory term meaning primarily a person of Italian descent, was entered in only two of the 1966 books; *New World* and *SCD* both called it *slang*; *SCD* added that it was "an offensive term," and *New World* called it "a vulgar term of prejudice and contempt." Again, *ACD* and *Seventh New Collegiate* did not list it. Of today's four leaders, only *New World II* does not list the word. *American Heritage II* describes it as *"Offensive Slang."* *Random House Revised* labels it *"Disparaging and Offensive,"* and *Ninth New Collegiate* says it is "usu. used disparagingly."

In 1966 *spi(c)(k)*, meaning "a Spanish-speaking person," appeared only in *SCD*, where it was labeled *"U.S. Slang"* and described as "an offensive term." Today three books (all but *New World II*) record the word, *American Heritage II* labeling it *"Offensive Slang,"* *Random House Revised* calling it *"Offensive,"* and *Ninth New Collegiate* saying "usu. taken to be offensive."

Hunky and its near neighbor *bohunk* are older terms that, like others in the group, seem to be disappearing from current use, except perhaps by speakers from the oldest generation. In 1966 three of the four leading college dictionaries had entries for each word. *ACD* labeled *hunky* *"U.S. Slang and Derogatory,"* and *bohunk,* *"U.S. Slang . . .* in contemptuous use." Today *Random House Revised* describes both words as "Disparaging." In 1966 *New World* gave both terms the same label and comment it gave *wop*; both were slang and each was "a vulgar term of prejudice and contempt." Today's *New World II* contains neither word. In 1966 *SCD* called both words *"U.S. Slang"* and, cross-referencing *hunky* to *bohunk*, said the terms were "offensive." *American Heritage* of course did not exist in 1966, but today's *American Heritage II* has an entry for *hunky*, which, curiously enough, it labels merely *"Slang,"* but not *"Offensive Slang"*! (Even more curious is that nightmare blunder that haunts every lexicographer: *American Heritage II*'s definition for *hunky* is simply "A bohunk," but there is no entry for *bohunk*. You see, there *was* an entry for *bohunk* in the 1981 New College Edition of *American Heritage*. But it was dropped in the 1982 *American Heritage II*, and the now useless entry for *hunky* was [alas] kept unchanged. Incidentally, in that 1981 entry for *bohunk*, the label was "*Slang*. . . . Used disparagingly"). Merriam's 1966 *Seventh New Collegiate* had no entry for either word, but today's *Ninth* has an entry for *hunky* (not for *bohunk*) and labels it "usu. used disparagingly." Definitions are usually much like *Ninth New Collegiate*'s, "a person of central or East European birth or descent," with the etymologies suggesting variants on *Hungarian* and *Bohemian* as likely sources for the words.

In these examples of older racially or ethnically offensive terms we can see slang behaving like slang; older words fall out of use and begin to disappear from all but the unabridged and historical dictionaries, often appearing with labels such as *archaic* or *obsolete*. Or, if they are deemed not quite obsolete, they are recorded in the college dictionaries, but with stiffer restrictive labels than ever before. The taboo against these kinds of words has become much stronger and more widely effective over the past twenty years; some of these words are not just *falling* out of use; most, in fact, are being *pushed* out, and pushed hard.

Except for *New World II*, the college dictionaries today seem usually to be taking the line that if the vulgate ethnic word is still in use, it ought be recorded and its status made unmistakably clear. And *New World II*, whose predecessor, *New World*, had some of the strongest and most unequivocal restrictive labels and comments when it did list many of these words, seems now to reflect an emotional-commercial judgment rather than a lexicographical one. It considers these words "the true obscenities" and on that basis will no longer give them space, not because they are obsolete but because they are obscene. But to hide your eyes and close your ears won't make the language (or much else) go away.

On getting back into touch with the language, I learned four important lessons about linguistic change and variation in our vulgarities and obscenities and about our attitudes toward them:

First, I learned that the long-lasting taboo on the use of sexual and excretory terms, particularly in mixed company, and especially as applied to the use of some of the functionally and semantically changed senses and combined forms of these terms, has weakened considerably. In their primary senses, these words certainly have not achieved acceptable status for all situations, nor are they soon likely to, but especially in figurative senses we find them today occurring in a much wider series of contexts both spoken and written, and we find them occurring in sexually mixed groups and in women's speech with much greater frequency than was true in 1966 and before. Only the older generations seem to retain most of their discomfort over breaches of this old taboo, and not all members of these generations retain uniformly conservative views.

Second, I learned that exactly the opposite change has affected the taboo against the use of racially and ethnically derogatory words. While I was away, this second taboo became much stronger and more fully effective than it had been in the early 1960s and before. In one sense this taboo has become even stronger than that hitherto strongest of all taboos for Standard English users: the taboo against using certain vulgate grammatical locutions that signal the low-class status of the inadvertent user. Today, society will often forgive (although it will not forget) an inadvertent double negative (*It don't make no difference*) combined with a failure of number concord or agreement between subject and verb. But great parts of society today will never forgive the use of an ethnic slurword such as *nigger* or *hymie-town*, however inadvertent.

Third, from these two lessons showing the weakening of one hitherto strong taboo and the increasing power of another originally not nearly so strong, I learned that those who view the future of the language gloomily because it appears that all the bars are either down or falling, because permissiveness is everywhere, are just plain wrong. The idea that many modern speakers, writers, and students of the language "are out to destroy . . . every vestige of linguistic punctilio, every surviving influence that makes for the upholding of standards, every criterion for distinguishing between better usages and worse" (Follett, 73) just isn't so. I consider these viewers-with-alarm needlessly gloomy: for one thing, their generalization is oversimple, far too sweeping, and therefore, at least in part, just plain wrong; for another, they need to be reminded that with language as with other manners, change is normal and inevitable. It is therefore almost as fruitless to fight the laws of gravity as it is to struggle against the inevitabilities of much linguistic change and variation. There never was a golden age.

The first taboo has weakened perceptibly over the past twenty years, and this observation does indeed support the wistful and the angry, illustrating as it does the sort of falling away of older standards that most who have invested in them hate to see. But the hugely increased effectiveness of the second taboo, the one against terms of racial and ethnic opprobrium, gives the lie to the idea that permissiveness is the only trend loose in the land. Our language will always serve our purposes—*all* our purposes.

Fourth, from this examination of the college dictionaries and their treatment then and now of the "bad" words, I learned once more—both from their changed editorial policies and from the details of individual entries—that we can indeed make useful generalizations about linguistic trends, but that we also must inform and correct our generalizations by the frequent close examination of individual words, meanings, and usages. And that to advise ourselves on what is acceptable where and when requires that we have both sound knowledge of the trends and the ability to evaluate each usage on its own merits. Even large gatherings of swallows do not necessarily make a summer, especially if calendar and thermometer disagree.

CHAPTER 7

Funny Talk from Elsewhere:
Regional Variation

One of the first things I noticed when I got back to the classroom was that my students talk today much the way my students talked twenty years ago. The sounds, the inflections, the syntax—all those bits and pieces of our speech that go together to make up the particular regional dialects we speak—sounded pretty familiar to me. That was a relief. I was delighted to find that I could still understand them and that they could still understand me: the noises we were making were and are still mutually intelligible.

Nonetheless, as I listen more carefully, I realize that there are differences between the way my students sounded twenty years ago and the way they talk today, and it's not solely a matter of slang and shifting taboos, either. Every time I listen, I can hear a few more changes, it seems. Some speech noises seem new or at least differently distributed. I hear some stress patterns that are new. I hear different inflections on some words. Some of the forms of words—*whom*, for example—seem to turn up much less frequently than they did. I seem to hear almost no subjunctives today except the stereotyped "If I were you." And some forms—*snuck* instead of *sneaked*, for example—that were not quite the thing before I left seem now at least to be tolerated if not (like *snuck*) fully accepted. There are new words and new meanings for old ones, too, of course; I expected that. But the other kinds of difference seem somehow more striking, more surprising. The numbers of these differences certainly aren't very great once I compare them with the almost countless facets of the language that appear not to have changed at all in twenty years. But there *are* differences, and they stand out clearly.

Language changes slowly; different aspects change at different rates, and each change is usually accomplished in tiny, incremental shifts. Changes in sounds, inflections, word orders, and in words and meanings are usually so slow as to be almost imperceptible from decade to decade. You can't see the hands of most clocks move while you watch them; only if you look away for a bit and then look back can you see that the hands have indeed moved. You can't see it happen; you can see only that it *has* happened. So it is with most linguistic change. Hence the curious advantage I find in having interrupted my close observation of American English for twenty years: now it's easier for me to see the results of those tiny, incremental changes than it is for those who've never been away.

Another help to observers of linguistic change is this: among the thousands of features that make up the various systems of a living language, most are shared by all the speakers of that language. The speaker of another regional or social dialect sounds odd to me, but actually, the noises he makes—the sounds, inflections, words, and their arrangements—are nearly all just like those I make; the bulk of what he says is what I would say too. Most of the *Oxford English Dictionary*'s words are just as much *my* vocabulary as they are Queen Elizabeth's; we speak them a bit differently, and once in a while we make them mean a bit differently, but the *boots*, *trunks*, *hoods*, and *bonnets* are really only a tiny fraction of the lexicon of English; like our different sound patterns—the queen's and mine—these differences are more amusing than troubling, more interesting than inconvenient.

When I listen to a stranger talking, it takes only a relative handful of different sounds or forms or patterns or words in his speech to trigger my judgment that his speech is different and that he "talks funny." So, as I began to listen professionally once more to my students, my colleagues, and others, I had little trouble picking up the differences.

Getting to know the twenty or thirty students in each of my first few semesters' classes reassured me immediately on one point about which I was curious: regional dialects. And what I've learned about Connecticut and this part of the Northeast illustrates what I suspect are similar forces at work on some of the other American regional dialects; hence my local observations may illuminate your own dialectal observations. I can still hear in each of my classes some of the sounds peculiar to each of the three regional dialects regularly heard in Connecticut, just as I could back in the early 1960s. Here and there I can hear an occasional Middle Atlantic or Midland or (rarely) Southern regional dialect sound, but those are oddities; most of my students today speak dialects that are some combination of these three: Eastern New England (sometimes called Coastal Northeastern), Northern, and Metropolitan New York. Yet as I listen I notice some differences between what I hear now of these regional dialects and what I used to hear from my classes twenty years ago. Perhaps the most striking difference is that fewer of my students today exhibit strong marks of either Eastern New England or Metropolitan New York dialect than would have been the case in similar classes in the early 1960s.

These differences appear to be of two sorts: first, there seem to be fewer speakers of either of these dialects in my classes than there were before and correspondingly more speakers of Northern dialect instead; second, most of those who do display features of either the Eastern New England or the Metropolitan New York dialect are rarely full-blown textbook examples. That is, although their Northern-speaking classmates and I can usually spot them easily, the fact is that phonological and other evidences of their dialects are much less pronounced (the pun of course is intentional) today than would have been typical twenty years ago. There are fewer speakers of those two dialects in my classes today, and most of those speakers display fewer and less strongly marked features of the two dialects.

Why should this be so? Here are some conjectures. First, it's possible that there really are fewer speakers of these two dialects in Connecticut today. It's conceivable that the Northern dialect is taking over, at least among college students. Certainly these dialects remain strong and vigorous at home in metropolitan Boston and metropolitan New York City, but the boundaries of the two dialects within Connecticut could be contracting. Or, Northerners could be submerging the other two dialects in their own territories within the state. Or, perhaps it's not the areas that have shrunk, but the populations *in* those areas. Or, perhaps this university simply doesn't have as many students as it did twenty years ago from Rhode Island and eastern Massachusetts and from New York City, West-chester County, Long Island, and northern New Jersey. All of these are plausible explanations for the change, at least at first glance. But how do they fit the facts?

Certainly northeastern Connecticut, where the state's Eastern New England dialect speakers can be found, continues to shrink in population: its agriculture and its old textile industry are nearly moribund, and much of it is, on balance, poor, have-not country, unlikely to send a high percentage of its children to a university. The chief problem with this hypothetical explanation for change over the last twenty years is that the demographic trend isn't really new. The area I'm discussing has been sparsely populated and fairly poor since the nineteenth century, and it seems likely that I would not have had very many students from that part of the state twenty years ago or even earlier.

More to the point, however, is the fact that this kind of explanation makes no sense at all when I try to apply it to the Metropolitan New York dialect. In Connecticut the Metro dialect is spoken in much of Fairfield County, the lower left-hand corner county that abuts New York's Westchester County and is often called New York City's bedroom because of the number of its residents who commute to Manhattan to work; the dialect also occurs in most of the shoreline towns to the east along Long Island Sound at least as far as New Haven. But this southwestern part of the state, particularly around the cities of Stamford, Greenwich, Danbury, Stratford, Bridgeport, and New Haven, is one of the two main population centers in the state (Greater Hartford, so-called, is the other), and it is the only area that is growing; Bridgeport is now the largest city in the state. Moreover, Fairfield County and the shoreline towns are well-heeled; some of the suburban towns, like their Westchester neighbors, are genuine Saxon cartoon country. Hence it is not surprising to learn that this university gets large numbers of students from this area, and that their numbers and the percentage of the total student body that they represent are increasing rapidly and have been doing so for most of the past twenty years. So here the demographic argument leads me to expect more, not fewer, Metropolitan New York dialect speakers in my classes—exactly the reverse of what I suspect to be true today.

Nor does the suspicion that there may be fewer students today from the out-of-state home territories of these two dialects hold up under scrutiny. Today there are nearly twice as many out-of-state residents in the freshman class as there were in 1966, and most of them come from one of four neighboring states, the very states where Eastern New England dialect (Massachusetts and Rhode Island) and Metropolitan New York dialect (New York and New Jersey) have their homes. So that's not a cause of the change in the campus dialectal mix. There must be better reasons than these. My best guess is that two sorts of what we might term *cosmopolitanism* (the opposite of *provincialism*, of which I'll speak in chapter 14) can help explain the changes I find in the regional dialect situation in my classes today.

First, the state of Connecticut is becoming more and more heterogeneous in its demographic mix. In a sense there is no longer a rural Connecticut; it is all either urban or suburban, and much of the population is originally from somewhere else—another town or the next county or another state. Especially in the thriving Fairfield County shoreline towns (midwesterners would call them *townships*), one gets the impression that nearly everyone has come from somewhere else, and if this isn't true of my students, it is almost literally true of their parents, many of whom live in that part of Connecticut but commute to New York to work. A very high percentage of the parents of my students from that southwestern part of the state are not "from" New England, and a fair number belong to that large group of corporation-driven nomads who were in Dallas for three years, in Chicago for five, and hope for San Francisco after a few more years in Darien or Westport. Thus the regional dialect mix in the southwestern part of the state is composed mainly of varieties of the Northern and Metropolitan New York dialects, but with generous sprinklings of nearly every other U.S. regional dialect as well.

The dialectal situation is such that the larger numbers of Northern speakers and the general strength of cultivated regional dialects from elsewhere have combined with certain attitudes toward the uncultivated Metro speaker and New York City native, whose speech (thanks to radio and television and the movies) has made him a cliché the country over, to wear away and perhaps even to stamp out some of the peculiarly Metropolitan features. The cabbie is perhaps the classic form of the cliché, as, for instance, in that Goodyear TV tire commercial of 1985: "Hiyuh, Vectuh! I'm

Nohm Shecktuh!" Some of these features are being softened and smoothed away by the Northern dialects surrounding them in Connecticut, much the way stones on beaches are smoothed and rounded and worn away by flowing water. This intermixing of the regional dialects is one sort of cosmopolitanism. When *The Linguistic Atlas of New England* was being compiled back in the 1930s, much of Connecticut was still rural, and it was still possible then for the atlas makers to find informants whose entire lives, including such formal education as they might have acquired, had taken place in the same small rural New England town. Today, cities, suburbs, supermarkets, and interstate highways are part of nearly everyone's life, just as are movies, radio, and television. These cosmopolitan influences are everywhere, and almost no one is untouched by them. Everybody has been to the city to shop, to see a hockey game, to visit the doctor, to have dinner, or to work. Nor is there any single huge city or metropolitan area to dominate all within and around it: Connecticut's cities are small; Bridgeport is largest, at 142,546. We're not hearing a single dialect. Today we've all heard and answered all sorts of dialects, not just those of relatives and neighbors. It's a very different sort of world, and in the aggregate, these influences have tended to wear down some of the features of regional dialects, even though they cannot destroy or remove them completely.

But there's also a second kind of cosmopolitanism that I believe bears on the matter of regional dialects today. In another way, my students now are much less parochial or provincial than were their parents twenty or more years ago when *they* were my students. For one thing, many more of today's students are the sons and daughters of people who attended college; not many could claim that distinction twenty years ago. Whatever cultivation and mobility this experience has added to the parents' formative influences on their children make a difference. It is also quite possible, and certainly more likely with each passing year, that today's student's father came from a different dialect area than did her mother, particularly if the two met in college. If the parents' parents met in high school or at a local factory or church, as would more likely have been the mode for grandparents of twenty years ago, then it's no wonder that the New Haven or Bridgeport sounds and locutions—partly metropolitan New York sounds and locutions, probably—were embedded in the speech of both and so were strongly evident in their children's speech. But their daughter married a man she met at college, a man reared in Hartford or Columbus or Denver, so *their* child (my student today) is bound to have fewer unmixed characteristics of Bridgeport or Hartford, Columbus, or Denver than have her parents. Where she comes from will be less obvious from her speech than her parents' origins will be from theirs. The signs will still be there for those who recognize them, but they will be far less obvious, and they will be a mixture.

So we can be certain, I think, that at least two forces have tended to knock off or smooth down some of the regional dialect features in the speech of my students today. The chances are good that they have been exposed from the beginning to more than one regional dialect, even in their own homes, and that they have heard in their formative years far less of *any* one regional dialect (and more of one or more others) than did their parents, just as the parents had heard less of any one dialect than had *their* parents. And there are few American dialects and almost no *cultivated* American dialects that today's radio- and TV-informed students have not heard at one time or another. This could not have been said of their parents at the same age, probably, and of their grandparents, certainly.

To these developments—the fact that today there's no farm to keep 'em down on, and the fact that today they've all seen Broadway, in the movies and on the tube if not in the flesh—we should add at least one other factor: the centralization of formal education, especially the development of the consolidated grade school and the comprehensive regional high school, the regional community college, and the colleges and universities, public and private, in state and out, which many more people today are likely to attend than was the case a generation ago. All of this centralization gives further impetus to the growth of dialectal cosmopolitanism. My twenty years away from professional observation of the language coincided with a sizable chunk of that change (most of the consolidated high schools in nonurban Connecticut were built after World War II), even though the process itself has been continuous at least since Connecticut began to become industrialized early in the nineteenth century.

Although I might hear little pure Eastern New England dialect in my classes today, I still find some features of it. Whereas in the early 1960s, in any given class of thirty students I might have had eight or nine who displayed at least some of the features of the dialect, plus one or two who displayed most of them, today I'm more likely to have three or four Eastern New England speakers at most, and only rarely do I find an unmixed exemplar. But I still can hear in every class at least some of the features of what the rest of the country usually thinks of as New England's dialect: that sometimes r-less, sometimes intrusive-r-bearing dialect with the funny Kennedy family vowels; to speakers of certain other regional dialects, it's the dialect that makes the phrase *law and order* sound like "lore 'n' awda," and the word *bath* like either "bawth" or "bahth." (Neither of these approximations is really like the vowel Eastern New England speakers have, but outlanders can rarely make speech noises they can't hear or discriminate; they hear only speech noises they can make themselves.) Most of my students today who have some of the sounds of this dialect have only very faint tinges of these sounds, and sometimes they have them in divided use: certain words, or in some circumstances the same words, will on one occasion reflect Eastern New England dialect, on another, Northern.

Some of the same modifications that have affected my students who are Eastern New England speakers have also affected those who are speakers of the Metropolitan New York dialect, which has its own version of r-lessness, its foreignisms such as glottal stop instead of the -t- in the middle of words like *bottle* and *little*, its "dis" and "dese" for *this* and *these*, its Bert Lahr–Barbra Streisand "noive" for *nerve*, its strong liprounding of the first vowel in words like *often* and *awful* (round your lips for the vowel of *who* and then say *awful* instead), and its fully exploded g's at the ends of -ing words, so that *singer* rimes with *finger*, and *Long Island* is pronounced "LonGIsland." The social message the Metro dialect seems to carry in the rest of the country is that it is "New York City speech," or "the way they talk in Brooklyn or the Bronx," even if the speaker is really from Bridgeport or New Haven. Given the outlander's general suspicion of worldly cabbies and violence in the subways, that may not be a wholly appealing message: "It's a great place to visit, but I wouldn't want to live there," goes the cliché. The dialect does not—at least outside New York City itself, and certainly not in its uncultivated versions—evoke images of the beautiful people or of wealth, "class," or power.

In genetic terms, one might say that when Metro speakers are mixed with fair numbers of speakers of other Northern dialects (as in much of southwestern Connecticut these days), so that the Metro speakers are no longer in the majority, the Metro dialect seems now to be recessive. One might hazard a similar observation about Eastern New England dialect south and west of the Greater Boston-Providence-Worcester triangle. In their home territories both dialects still thrive, although some cultivated speakers, even in New York City itself, feel a social stigma may be attached to the Metro speech. More of that in a moment. The fact remains that Mayors Edward Koch of New York and Ray Flynn of Boston both need speak only a sentence or two on a national television newsclip to have listeners from anywhere in the country know at once which city each of them comes from, whether they recognize the mayors or not.

At any rate, both these dialects seem somehow to be receding a bit from the territories they once held within the state of Connecticut. Perhaps if there is a stigma attached to either or both, it is that each marks the speaker's place of origin more clearly and narrowly for other Americans than do most other regional dialects. Charleston, South Carolina, speech is very special too, and so is Nashville speech, but few Americans from other parts of the country can distinguish the first from the speech of Atlanta or New Orleans or the second from that of Dallas or Tulsa. Anyone from Minneapolis or Los Angeles or any of the cities named above can spot a speaker of Metro dialect as a New Yorker and a speaker of Eastern New England dialect as a Bostonian, or thinks he can, and that in effect nails the speaker to his point of origin; all that is needed is the clear dialect, and the speaker becomes to his outlander listeners a cliché—and a geographically pinpointed one at that. The South, on the other hand, whether we're listening to Southern or South Midland dialects, is a large and varied place. Lyndon Johnson and Jimmy Carter spoke different dialects, but without other information, most Americans from the northern part of the country could not have been certain about what state to assign these dialects to.

Perhaps there is something in all of that to explain the diminishing amount of Eastern New England and Metropolitan New York dialect I can hear in my classes today. Generally, we're talking of young people who are or who hope to be upwardly mobile (to use the current jargon). It may also be true that some of the stigmata,* real or imagined, stem from more deep-seated prejudice among outlanders; it may not be just a matter of wishing to seem a citizen of the world rather than a peasant from a narrow place. It has been alleged of Metro speech that it can evoke anti-Semitic sentiments among some Midland listeners. And it is also alleged that to some bigots from other dialect areas, Eastern New England speech suggests Roman Catholicism—a curious allegation, despite the Kennedy family, given the long and powerful influence of Boston Protestant Brahmanism on midwestern education and culture from Emerson (at least) to World War II. These are of course very difficult allegations to judge. Nonetheless, for whatever reasons, we must recognize that to be different from others can sometimes be perilous, especially among the fearful. Dialects can cause us to differ.

At any rate we have evidence that the dialect of Metropolitan New York seems to some of its own speakers to carry enough of a pejorative aura with it that they seek to lose the features of that speech so that the dialect won't limit their social and economic mobility, even within New York City itself. An article reprinted from the *Chicago Tribune* in the *Hartford Courant* for 1 July 1984 (H-1) describes the popularity of a four-week course on Standard American Speech, offered by a New York Center for Speech Arts, with private tutoring "for those who want to sound more like Edwin Newman and less like Phil Foster." Many of the students (says the article) sign up because they have trouble getting ahead professionally when they sound like stage New Yorkers. Such evidence,

---

*My use of the Latin plural form here will for some readers seem self-consciously learned, but although many would prefer the normal English plural, *stigmas*, both the "conservative" *American Heritage II* and the "liberal" *Ninth New Collegiate* report both plurals, listing *stigmata* first (that order means only that both are perfectly acceptable forms, but that if there is any difference, it is that the one listed first may seem to occur more frequently). My own guess is that using it figuratively as I did in the passage, but with the explicit suggestion of scars or marks, seems to call for the old Christian plural, with its referent of visible wounds. One thing you might like to consider is whether, if you'd been writing it, you might deliberately have ducked the issue by choosing the singular.

admittedly only anecdotal, underscores for me this particular difference between the language situation I left in the early 1960s and the one I've returned to today: the regional dialect picture in the Northeast is changing, especially in southern New England, and there are some new forces at work, especially on Metro dialect, forces apparently aimed at leveling and homogenizing. One can imagine similar forces at work in places such as Florida, North Carolina's research triangle, the Sunbelt cities like Atlanta, Houston, Dallas, and Phoenix, and the entire Pacific slope. The Cronkites and Rathers may have had something to do with it too, not directly influencing, but indirectly stimulating many to lose their localisms if they can (though Rather's South Midland dialect is often quite obvious to Northern speakers).

What all the evidence shows, I think, is that the world of *The Linguistic Atlas of New England*—and probably the worlds of other linguistic atlases as well—has faded a great deal. It's not that we have fewer regional dialects, nor is there any suggestion that we're all moving in our speech toward some sort of homogenized "General American" dialect. * Some dialect features, particularly some of the sounds and some of the morphology (the forms of words), are readily apparent: where I use *dived* as the past tense most of the time, New Englanders almost always use *dove*. But among cultivated speakers generally, and among those others who at least try to emulate them when possible, many dialect features have become—the pun again, but true—less pronounced. Yet in this very same country, as chapter 14 will suggest, we can see the effects on dialect of the increasing provincialism of our large inner cities. It seems to me that both the new cosmopolitanism and this new kind of provincialism are important developments to watch.

---

*Quite the reverse, according to sociolinguists who work on northeastern urban dialects. Most see the city dialects—especially the nonstandard dialects—diverging more and more from the standard dialects of the rest of the nation. Isolation, especially in our large inner cities (New York, Philadelphia, Baltimore, and Boston have been much studied), is fostering these growing divergences. For an excellent brief account, see William K. Stevens, "Stronger Urban Accents in Northeast Are Called Sign of Evolving Language," 36.

CHAPTER 8

More Change and Variation

Think a bit about these utterances; turn them over on your tongue and savor the various kinds of social information they give you. I've already touched on the first three:

1. "I'm going to wash your mouth out with soap! Nice boys don't use words like that!"

Clearly, mothers don't intend to tolerate obscenities and vulgarities in the mouths of their young sons.

2. "I just love to hear that girl on TV talk about 'a rainy naht in Jawjuh.'"
3. "I think his accent is cute. I bet he's Australian."

These latter two, of course, express some judgments on regional variation—on regional dialects both inside and outside the United States. But these only begin to suggest the range and power of linguistic variation. And nearly all my questions about speech that sounded different or writing that looked different from what I had been hearing and reading twenty years ago bore on some aspect of linguistic change and variation.

Consider these utterances:

4. "Gramps has been fly fishing for more than sixty years, and when he really gets going on it, only another fly fisherman can tell what he's talking about."
5. "He's very polite, but you can tell he's never had much education; his grammar is awful."
6. "I could tell by your voice when you answered the phone that you had someone else there in the room with you."
7. "Where on earth did you pick up that expression? What in the world does it mean?"

8. "Reverend Johnson talks like a book; he must be a very smart man."

Each of these five describes or illustrates at least one other kind of *linguistic variation*, at least one other way in which a language gets adjusted, depending on the speaker, the speaker's background, the situation, the audience, and the purpose of the utterance. And there are other variations—spelling, for example—peculiar to the written language. All linguistic variations are of course differences in sound, form, or some other facet of the language, and some of them, through many repetitions in many voices, may become "permanent" linguistic changes—permanent, that is, until the next Van Winkle awakes to discover that even the "permanent" can change.

If you say or write something differently from the way I would do it, or differently from the way I expect you to do it, I'll notice the differences. If they're large or numerous or shocking, I may notice *only* the differences, and so miss the substance of what you say. And in any event, depending upon our relative roles and relationships—on whether you're bigger or smaller than I, I'll either scramble to imitate your variations, or—if I have the power or think I do—I'll criticize or perhaps even punish you for varying from what I expect. For these reasons, linguistic variation is an important subject; its details are matters I had to look into right away.

Any kind of linguistic variation has the potential for putting backs and voices up almost anywhere within the population. One sort of variation, the use of obscenities and vulgarities, can evoke the parental response of the previous example 1. As I said in chapters 4, 5, and 6, obscenities pose some special problems, but this particular example also suggests the differing responses *any* given locution, obscene or not, can sometimes evoke from the different generations of listeners. Examples 2 and 3 suggest that the speakers enjoy hearing these particular "foreign" regional dialects; but for every person who is favorably disposed, there can be others who find the same regional dialect funny rather than charming, and still others who find it irritating or maddening. Here we might recall what we said in chapter 7 about the anti-Semitism that

Metropolitan New York dialects may sometimes evoke elsewhere in the country. Examples 4 and 7 suggest how easily our choices of words and expressions, deliberate or inadvertent, can shut others out of our group's talk. Examples 5 and 8 underscore in different ways—5 in usage and 8 in syntax and choice of vocabulary—the wide range of social judgments that can result from linguistic variation. And example 6 reminds us of the truly complex ways in which we may unconsciously adapt our speech to the audience and the situation; much of the time it's not what we say or even the words we use—it's quite literally *how* we say it that makes the difference.

Let me add just a bit more about regional variations: even though they *can* evoke negative responses, in fact it appears that of themselves they don't do the damage; they need help, either from being combined with some social variation—substandard syntax, for example—or from some extralinguistic force such as dress or manners. In the end, whether we're hearing presidents of the United States, listening to Dolly Parton or Roger Miller, or watching *Dallas* or a Pepperidge Farm television commercial, most cultivated speakers of the language will agree that in the United States today, any moderately cultivated regional dialect is as good outside its home grounds as is any other. One need only compare the speech of Franklin Roosevelt, Harry Truman, Dwight Eisenhower, John Kennedy, Lyndon Johnson, Richard Nixon, Gerald Ford, Jimmy Carter, and Ronald Reagan, the presidents whose voices nearly every adult has heard either live or recorded, to realize that although each carried the marks of his region in his speech, these marks in and of themselves almost never caused misunderstanding among listeners outside his dialectal region. Only rarely did any of his regional dialectal differences evoke scorn or hatred from speakers of other dialects *except* as a reinforcement of existing political or social disagreement or dislike. If you disliked Lyndon Johnson, then of course you didn't like the way he talked.

In my northeastern Ohio youth, for example, Franklin Roosevelt's cultivated lower Hudson Valley speech was to all my neighbors a clearly audible sign that he was regionally and socially different. Democrats whose dialect it was not might not have been amused, impressed, or even awed by it, but Republicans frequently found it snobbish or otherwise hateful. Those of us who are old enough can remember the comic mimicry of the period, such as "I hate wah, Eleanoah hates wah. . . ." But we all understood him.

Perhaps my present neighbors here in Connecticut were most sorely tested for dialectal prejudice during the Johnson and Carter terms: the South has been judged by the Northeast more harshly and longer than other regions, perhaps for its slavery, its agrarian backgrounds, and its religious fundamentalism, but more likely for the whole range of issues surrounding the Civil War. The South's dialects have until lately suffered in the North as symbols of these other matters. But as hillbillies have gone Hollywood, and as the Bible Belt has become the Sunbelt, so more recently have manufacturing, money, opportunity, and power appeared to move South. So too the attitudes toward its dialects have begun to change; whether the dialects suggest the studied rural innocence of Nashville's country music, the slickness and display of the Houston Astrodome and Texas Stadium, the tawdry attractiveness of New Orleans' Bourbon Street, or the sophistication of the Atlanta sky-line, they now let us in full truth make the statement we made above: "Most cultivated speakers . . . will agree that . . . any moderately cultivated regional dialect is as good outside its home grounds as is any other." If the Metropolitan New York dialect is in some ways an exception, we should remember that it may also be in some trouble at home too, a development that seems relatively new and therefore worth keeping track of.

The generalization is by no means a new point. British commentators have noted almost from the beginning of their investigative travels in this country, especially in the nineteenth century and thereafter, that regional differences in the language of Americans seem neither to erect bars to communication nor to stigmatize their speakers when they speak a cultivated version of their regional dialect outside their home territory. Britons still cannot say the same of some of their own regional dialects; it's a peculiarly American English matter. And it seems to be even clearer today than twenty years ago.

Then there are the linguistic variations that mark social class dialects. Judgments such as those explicit in example 5 ("He's very polite, but you can tell he's never had much education; his grammar is awful.") have long been a feature of this democratic society.

"Spanglish" and the various northern urban black dialects are only the latest in a long string of vulgates—the great American Vulgate, as Mencken called it—in which people from the lower end of the socio-economic-educational scale express themselves. These vulgate dialects display morphological, phonological, syntactic, and lexical differences of all sorts, and many of these differences specifically mark their users as belonging to a lower class. A *he don't*, a *he not here*, a *she be workin' steady now*, an *I ain't seen him today*, or an unconscious double negative—all these can bring class and sometimes race prejudice into play.

But outside the schools, where efforts to instill and sometimes to exemplify the ideals of upward social mobility are supposed to be continuous, these social class kinds of linguistic variation seem to me to have contributed surprisingly little to recent changes in the full language.

What have struck me on my return as the liveliest contests over linguistic variation are the quarrels over current usage waged by users of Standard or nearly Standard English against one another. Here the middle and upper classes are intermixed. And here, surely, are the most vigorously contested and highly publicized of the struggles over linguistic change and variation. Perhaps they were as visible and lively before the early 1960s, but I don't remember them that way. Certainly the intemperance and decibel levels and the quality of the occasional wit and humor, if not of the erudition displayed, began to increase noticeably after *Webster III* appeared in 1961. But on my return, I've felt that the arguments now continue at much more "popular" levels, not just at the old academic and literary-critical levels of the earlier part of this century, when the world was ruled by Fowlers and Websters and if you weren't satisfied with a Fowler or a *Webster II* as the arbiter of linguistic taste and correctness, the fault was almost certainly yours, and the question probably not worth raising.

Evidence of the liveliness of the action these days seems to be everywhere. All will take exception to nearly any variation from their own practice they encounter in the language of others whom they consider their equals or something less. Some are timorous and look for support before attacking, but others leap fearlessly into the fray: clearly, these deviants, whoever they are, ought be made to meet their judges' own (better) standards. It's wonderful. The wrong case in a pronoun use, as in *They asked Mary and I* or *Us girls will get the dinner,* variant vulgate versions of a couple of preterits or past participles, such as *He's growed a foot since I seen him last* or *They drug the pond where they thought he'd drownded,* elicit almost equal scorn, despite the fact that while many Standard English speakers regularly get entangled in the cases of pronouns, especially in speech and particularly in constructions with compound subjects or objects, they rarely make vulgate mistakes in the preterits of strong verbs. (You can tell that Standard speakers rarely make that kind of mistake because the deliberate use of a vulgate preterit for comic effect is a frequent Standard practice, as in *Who'd a thunk it?* Only people confident of their control and confident too that listeners will know the error is deliberate and funny, not inadvertent and embarrassing, will take those kinds of chances. Most of the time, standard users play only sure things.)

Of course, certain errors in concord and agreement, like those of vulgate verb forms (*Fred and his uncle goes to every game; We come as soon as we could*), have long been clear marks of lower social class, leading to inferences about the speaker's probable lack of formal education, low level of occupation, and lack of economic and political or social power.

But really, in these kinds of usage issues, case in some pronouns aside, there is relatively little disagreement among Standard speakers. Nearly all agree on the prohibition of the most obvious of the forms of the vulgate. But they disagree among themselves on many other matters, sometimes nervously and tentatively, sometimes arrogantly and self-righteously.

The erosion of the subjunctive in all but a few situations (we keep it in *I move that the secretary cast one ballot for . . .* , and in *If he were here, he'd . . .* , but most of us would say and write *If he arrives* [not *arrive*] *on time, we'll . . .*"); or the dwindling of most oral and many written *whom* forms not tucked in directly behind prepositions; or the waning of the genitive-before-gerund construction (*I dislike him* [instead of *his*] *complaining*)—all these bring divided usage, divided judgments, and therefore argument. Many such items are either in divided usage—that is, sizable groups of Standard users champion each of the possible options, with the groups of defenders changing in size and composition as the audience, the situation, and the purpose of the utterance vary—or these items will have nearly achieved or nearly lost status with everybody who is anybody. In these last instances we find some of the loudest quarrels, especially when a locution appears to have become acceptable within the standard language for all but the purest of the purists or for all but the most formal of audiences, situations, and purposes. Ordinarily, such quarrels don't drag on very long; occasionally, they last for generations; hopefully (see p. 128), we can avoid having very many of those.

We can trace much of the unhappiness expressed by purists, and others who would defend the language from the rest of us, to two kinds of linguistic variation in particular. In my view, today's noisiest battles over usage are being fought not between the regions or the social classes, but between small constituencies of specialists and the general population—that's one set of skirmishes—and between the older and the younger generations.

A good deal of it comes from the variations—particularly in vocabulary—that reflect the special interests of one expert constituency or in-group—such as the fly fishermen in example 4. But even more uproar and unhappiness and viewing-with-alarm are caused, I think, by those linguistic variations that reflect the differing practices of youth (and innovation and freshness) and those of age (and experience and tradition)—such as are illustrated in examples 1 (the mouthwashing threat) and 7 ("Where . . . did you pick up that expression?"). We'll devote the rest of this chapter to the trades and vocations and their argots and jargons. The generations, then, can have a chapter unto themselves, as I think they clearly warrant.

First, the specialists—the fly fishermen and the other tradesmen and professionals, the cliques and tongs, the clubs and cabals. The jargon of sports fans and players, the cant of the underworld and other subcultures, and the argot of the trades, professions, and other close-knit constituencies are today being snapped up much more quickly than ever before for trial use by the general population, including many speakers of Standard English. Communications—radio, television, and motion pictures especially, with their ability to show us how all sorts of people speak in all sorts of real and imagined situations—may well be the chief causes of the speedier movement of argot from its place of origin in the smaller group to acceptance as slang, and then later to acceptance as standard or to total rejection even as slang, by the larger speech community. These adoptions of terms that have belonged to a special constituency, together with the semantic and functional shifts that often affect such terms after the move, displease two groups of people.

Attempts to move such terms into general use often anger both those within the group whose lexicon has been plundered and those conservative outsiders who devoutly wish the word had remained in the relative obscurity of its origin, instead of befouling the standard language. Both sides see this borrowing as the debasement of "their" language. Consider how quickly in these days, when TV cops* talk with apparently total authenticity every night in the week, the general society picks up the drug culture's jargon: *coke, hash, shooting-up, head shop* (note how antique some of these sound already!), and the like. Every few months there are new coinages within the drug subculture to replace those terms that, in the ears of their inventors on the street, have been sullied and ruined by being taken over by the police, the press, the entertainment industry, and the general public. The mysteries of all sorts of tight little cults are constantly being exposed and "blown" by this means: *chop shop*, the clandestine workshop where thieves strip stolen cars for their parts, is already in the newspapers, though not yet in even the latest college dictionary. Think of the way we adopt sports terms and sporting figures of speech, terms such as *to fake* or *fake out*, meaning "to elude by deceiving," so that in the end it turns out that teachers can be said to fool their students just as halfbacks fool safety men or forwards, goalies. Note how universally *to strike out* can mean "to fail." Or note how we stretch the meanings of medical (*My car has cancer of the fenders*) and psychiatric terms (*She has a phobia about red sweaters* or *He's getting paranoid about his serve*) to fit more general purposes. Or consider how we stretch the application of theatrical slang (a *smash* or a *hit*) already borrowed from elsewhere so that it will describe something else entirely. And think how we generalize military terms such as *dud* or respecialize astronomical terms such as

---

*Ninth New Collegiate offers no usage label, but American Heritage II and Random House Revised call *cop* "Informal"; New World II says it's "slang." *Police* and *policemen* seemed too stuffy for my needs here. How did it strike you? Too unbuttoned?

superstar and *nova* and *galaxy* for use in the world of entertainment.

Many of us have picked up for reapplication to other matters some of the real and invented terms used by Le Carré's Smiley and his people;* we know about *moles* and we even begin to think they are found not only in romances of international espionage, but also in our own circles, for less nefarious but still undesirable reasons. We pop such words into the regular vocabulary as slang at first, and some of them ultimately disappear without a trace, while still others—sometimes with surprising rapidity—achieve full acceptability in the standard lexicon. Golf borrowed its *par* from the terminology of monetary policy, but we've all used the term much more frequently in a more general sense as we discuss our health or lack of it. The speed of such change is sometimes almost incredible. Last year I heard David Marr, a golf professional and television commentator, refer to the disastrous eight scored by a young professional golfer on a pivotal hole near the end of a tournament as a *snowman*. The figure is graphic, but I'd never heard it used in golf before, despite having scored enough eights in my day to have provided ample opportunity. Yet within the past two weeks, both on the course and off, I've heard the term used several times for the score of eight—still in golf. But quite possibly tomorrow it may be used for the score of eight in some other game, or simply for the number itself, game or not.

The problem is that not everyone appreciates the prospect of such rapid change. Many speakers of Standard English adopt slang words quickly, easily, without cavil of any sort. Some go even further and deliberately seek out slang and adapt it to their own purposes, just as they ape modish dress and modish manners, and for the same reasons. But others get angry and resentful of change and fight it wherever they can: conservative speakers of the standard language, who usually dislike most innovation, and conservatives of another sort, who simply wish to keep their argot for their own special purposes within their own particular mystery or in-group. What usually happens after such takeovers, of course, is that the

*Good accounts of Le Carré's contributions are in *Verbatim*, Spring and Autumn 1982 issues; Victor Lasseter provides an introduction and lexicon, Donald R. Morris a supplementary discussion.

in-group will quickly create a new argot term to replace the old one now soiled and stretched out of shape by being made into slang in the grubby hands of outsiders. But irritation persists.

So the trades and professions and other constituencies such as students and street gangs, bankers and ballplayers, cartographers and con men turn out to be both the creators of much argot and the victims of the persistent pilferage and fencing of that argot as the slang of the open market. (None of the latest college dictionaries gives a restrictive label to this sense of *fence*, which is a classic bit of criminal argot from the seventeenth century in Britain.) Such stealing and purveying, together with the vigorous efforts of purists outside the group to prevent the stolen goods from being fenced and peddled abroad, plus the equally vigorous efforts of the originators to hang onto their creations, provide us with one of what I see as the two most active battle grounds for American usage today. It's a battleground where words are captured and changed into new shapes and services, a process as old as language itself. But the difference today seems to be that thanks to our new technologies for communicating with each other, particularly those that have increased our ability to communicate orally, the process seems to go faster now than ever before. California's Valley girls had invented and then dropped their *gross me out to the max* long before the national news magazines could pass the locution on to their East Coast elders. The pattern of change is not different from what it was when I drifted off, but the speed of change I found when I returned seems considerably greater.

CHAPTER 9

The Generations in Conflict

James Thurber (in his famous cartoon sequence, "The War between Men and Women") and several other thoughtful observers have suggested that the most pervasive, monumental, and longest running of all human contests over manners is the battle of the sexes. They may be right, because that affray has certainly had a good deal of direct influence on American English over the past twenty years, as I discovered on my return to my trade. Actually, I'd noticed some of it before, even during my slumber: sometimes feminists' outrage at certain of the language's forms and customs was loud enough to wake the deepest of sleepers. No question, the battle of the sexes merits a chapter all its own. But that's the next chapter.

You see, I think the greatest battle of all is not between the sexes but between the generations. Specifically, I believe that the younger and the older generations are even more active combatants over the language and its use than are either the trades and professions or the sexes. I'm persuaded that the battleground whereon the older generations try to preserve what they think they've thus far managed to keep relatively unsullied by the intrusions and depredations of the young is the most active battlefield in all of American English usage. The results, it seems to me, are much more sweeping than the effects of the struggles of the trades and between the sexes. It's on this field that the younger generations try to hurry change along, to speed it up, as a part of their effort to win their own turf for their own usages, only to find in this aging but youth-worshiping society that as soon as they have invented a new term, created a new meaning, or established a new function for a word, some members of an older generation pounce at once on the novelty and adapt it to their own use, just as rapidly as the 1960s generation of over-thirty untrustworthies appropriated the jeans, beads, beards, and granny glasses of the youth of that time. The older generations, if they are not the members viewing with alarm and trying to prevent change, are busy co-opting, almost as fast as the young can invent them, such uniforms of dress, language, and other manners as they can find to help set themselves apart from their chronological peers and attach themselves instead to a more youthful constituency, which really doesn't want the middle-aged as members. So on this battleground it is fathers against sons, mothers against daughters, teachers against students, and the complacently middle-aged, the grandparents, and the truly elderly against them all. Then for a final complication we have to realize that included among those who are the most conservative, most rigorous defenders of some parts of the linguistic status quo are also some of the most zealous appropriators of the language of the young; we do indeed contain multitudes.

There are other illustrations of the generational differences, certainly. We need to delineate as many as four or five groups. First, there are *the pliant very young*, the small children, who embrace as good and worthy of imitation all the manners their parents and siblings display; they do not question. Next, there are *the unpliant young*, the student generation and its slightly older brothers and sisters, trying hard in their upward mobility to be a multitude themselves. They struggle to imitate and yet be different from the staid older world. Third, there are *the undecided middle-aged*, some of them conservative some of the time, particularly in their roles as parents, and all of them uncomfortable most of the time. And fourth, there are *the entrenched elderly* (who include some of the *decided middle-aged*), who not only know that they are right, but *must* reject any opinion not their own, since to accept any other view might imply that they've worshiped the wrong gods, followed the wrong leaders, held the wrong values, and so wasted their lives. Each of these groups plays its separate, distinct role in the struggle over usage, and that the several roles are different ensures that the language will change: the unpliant young will invent, the entrenched elderly will bewail or condemn, the undecided middle-aged will rush distractedly from one camp to the other, and the pliant young will trustingly imitate whatever they hear from all the others.

Now we'll look at a usage problem or two that will illustrate the divisions between the generations and some of the changes that those divisions have worked on the language over the past twenty years. I've already reported that the taboo on foul language, especially the excremental and sexual terms which were so long and so rigorously restricted to male society in its own lairs, has been relaxed for whole segments of society. The unpliant young in particular have shocked their elders by using in mixed company words that the older men use regularly in all-male situations, but only occasionally and usually inadvertently in front of women with any claim to respectability. Nor were such words ever before permitted in the presence of the pliant young.

The change, quite shocking at first both to the entrenched elderly and to the undecided middle-aged, began of course when my own generation returned from World War II, a bit freer with (or less able to control) some of the all-purpose four-letter words we had used freely during our years in the service. But most of us quickly clapped on the taboo when we got back home.

Then, in the 1960s, the Berkeley free speech movement and its followers stimulated the unpliant young to change. Deliberately and with all the shocking power they could muster, they startled most of us with words that, while we knew them well enough, we had seldom heard before in mixed company, particularly not in the mouths of women and children "of our kind." And on the campus, which was a special venue for all of this, as well as in the great world outside, some of their elders from the undecided middle-aged group began to ape the youth whose apparent liberation they so envied. Usually self-consciously, often absurdly, and generally with minimal imagination or daring, they too began to help break down the taboo, as we have seen in chapter 5. And at the same time as this taboo on such obscenities was falling, another was becoming infinitely stronger. First the idealistic unpliant young and then the undecided middle-aged generation became more sensitive to the changing social scene and with greater firmness than ever before clamped down what has now become an almost unbreakable taboo for all speakers of Standard English and for most speakers of other levels of American English as well. This is the taboo against the use of such terms of racial and ethnic opprobrium as *nigger* and *kike* and *spic*.

Today these terms are almost wholly excised from the Standard speaker's active vocabulary (and many of the young have never even heard of some of the older terms). Even Archie Bunker must be careful now. The ethnic joke and much of the language that so often it employs have had to go underground in nearly all cultivated levels of society, and in many more modest levels too; many Standard speakers today consider these terms unspeakable even underground. This turnabout is most remarkable, and it too is reflected in the differences between the generations more than it is in regional or even social class differences. Many an undecided middle-ager today is fully decided on this issue and cringes when he hears *his* elders still using terms even as relatively innocuous as *colored* (for *black*) was until the 1960s. Further, as parents these middle-agers rush nervously to correct any inadvertent imitation of grandpa by the pliant young, if grandpa doesn't know better than to use such terms.

There are other signs of generational difference, some of them fairly cacophonous, in the usages that reflect the new sensitivity of women to the names others call them or to the names they call themselves (we'll say more of this in chap. 10). Just as undecided men with thickening middles and thinning hair are occasionally shocked at being cursed or mocked for opening a door for an unpliant young woman, so there is similar shock among the entrenched elderly of both sexes when they discover what unpliant youth and some of its imitators consider at best an unappreciated quaintness in the term *lady* or *ladies*. Or consider the real anger evoked in some women by use of the term *girls* to refer to women of any age. I know an eighty-eight-year-old lady who is really baffled by that one, since she and "the girls" in her Tuesday afternoon bridge club have been referring to themselves as "the girls" for nearly sixty years. She would find her granddaughter's sensitivity on this point both absurd and puzzling, whether the latter had ever seen the old syndicated cartoon entitled "The Girls" or not.

The point is that it is the struggle between the middle-aged and the unpliant young, between parents and children, between teachers and students, with entrenched elderly grandparents glooming hopelessly or fulminating angrily in the background at what they see as failures in *all* the generations younger than they, that appears to me to be the busiest proving ground for much American English usage today. That's where the action is.

The *American Heritage Dictionary*'s much-vaunted panel of usage experts, most of them justly famed but on the average late middle-aged even in 1969 when *American Heritage* first appeared, is, in the most recent edition (*American Heritage II*, 1982), still proudly touted by editor and publisher for its advice on the usage of many items. Yet since all those listed as panel members in the front matter of this latest edition presumably helped form the usage notes printed in it, we should observe that their average age in 1986, four years after the second edition appeared, would be (if all were still alive) about seventy years. That such members of the entrenched elderly generation do indeed have an inordinate amount of leverage on the language, especially on the written language, is not surprising. Most of the panel members have written a great deal and had it published; most have solid literary, editorial, or journalistic reputations. But it is also a fact that although this culture is aging, it is also a youth-worshiping culture, and the elderly are by no means setting all the standards for social behavior, including use of language, even though many of them *wish* they were, and some of them may even *believe* they are.

Further, a comparison of dictionary entries of twenty years ago and those of today for several vexed usages illustrates that in many instances, conservatives like *American Heritage II*'s panel sometimes give advice that is useful primarily for those who hope to please an audience that includes or may be dominated by the entrenched elderly. Knowledge of what that may require is very useful to any writer or speaker, but simple "do this, not that" advice is insufficient and possibly even dangerously inaccurate, particularly for those for whom "talking like a book" may not provide sufficient flexibility to meet the demands of the more diversified audiences many writers and speakers hope to please. Those who set the pace for the usage of much of society in many of its utterances, written or spoken, are considerably younger than sixty-eight, as we can learn by examining our newspapers and magazines, attending our theaters and cinemas, listening to our disc jockeys and talk show hosts on the radio, and watching our anchormen, weatherwomen, and sportscasters on television.

Since my return to teaching, what's struck me so forcibly about the language is that the generations seem to have become even more important to usage than they were twenty years ago when I turned away. They've always been strong forces in questions of usage, but today they may well have become the most important: of all the interlocking constituencies each of us belongs to, our generation may contribute most significantly to our decisions about using the language. Let's consider a few of the details that lead me to that generalization.

Take *contact* as a verb. In 1934 *Webster II* was very firm; any use of *contact* as a verb, transitive or intransitive, was "Slang." Since then opinions have changed considerably, but the generations have seldom been in full agreement. Indeed, even though it is clear that today the issue has been decided, and *contact* is an accepted Standard English verb, it is also clear that some who refuse to accept the decision will die before they yield. Strong stuff.

Of the college dictionaries available in 1960, most agreed that use of *contact* as a verb was pretty widespread. But except for *New World* (1960), all the good college dictionaries gave it some sort of restrictive usage label. *ACD* and *Sixth New Collegiate* called it *"colloquial,"* and Funk and Wagnalls' *College Standard Dictionary* (1956) labeled it "popular," which meant that at best it *wasn't* very popular with at least some people in some situations. In her 1962 compilation, *Current American Usage* (60–61), Margaret Bryant reported, "Contact as a verb occurs in colloquial and informal usage," a statement supported by the several studies she cited. The newest dictionary on my desk when I left teaching was the Funk and Wagnalls *Standard College Dictionary*, published by Harcourt, Brace and World in 1963. *SCD* reported that *contact's* transitive meaning, "to get in touch with (someone)," was "Informal," but commented further: "This informal usage, regarded with disfavor by some, is widely used." The handwriting was on the wall.

Nonetheless, most of us who finished graduate school and began to teach college English about five or six years after the end of World War II were usually careful to avoid using *contact* as a verb when we were in school, regardless of which side of the lectern we were on. We tried never to use it in classroom discussions with our own teachers, and we all edited it out of our writing if we could. All of us knew that our graduate professors, like many of their peers in the great world outside, considered the verb *contact* a shibboleth that could be used to expose someone not a master of good English.

So, in turn, we tried to set a good example for our own students (when we remembered to), even though for most of them the prohibition was a brand new idea; many of us of course were unable to control the usage in conversation with our peers *or* our students.

By 1963 *Seventh New Collegiate*, like its parent *Webster III* in 1961, had dropped all usage labels for the verb *contact*. The Merriam editors concluded that *contact* was being used nearly everywhere without problem. But the older generations, especially the entrenched elderly, had by no means all accepted it, and if they did recognize that the verb was spreading all around them, many were still fighting at least to keep it out of formal written English. So, in 1969, *American Heritage* fought back against the "permissive" Merriam views with a usage note firmly declaring that the word "meaning to get in touch with, is widely used but still not appropriate to formal contexts, according to 66 per cent of the Usage Panel."

But that the battle was already beyond retrieval was obvious, and final confirmation is in the 1983 *Ninth New Collegiate*'s usage note, wherein the Merriam editors make clear their decision that in such vexed usage issues as this one, remaining silent (as their *Webster III* and *Seventh* and *Eighth New Collegiates* had done) is not quite the thing after all. "A few stalwart defenders of the language still object to the use of *contact* as a verb, esp. in sense 2b [to get in communication with ⟨~ your local dealer⟩]. But most commentators concede that it has become established as standard." That this is a sound conclusion is grudgingly acknowledged by the revised note in *American Heritage II* (1982): "*Contact* (verb), meaning to get in touch with, is widely used but is still considered inappropriate to formal use by a majority of the Usage Panel." One wonders whether that 66 percent majority has dwindled to a bare majority, or whether the note ought to have added "when we asked them thirteen years ago for our 1969 edition." The truth is that the remaining voices still raised against *contact* as a verb, both on *American Heritage*'s panel and in the rest of the American English world, are at best few in number, exceedingly mature, and most of them probably downright quavery.

Yet other lexicographical conservatives continue to give similarly aged advice; the 1980 *Oxford American Dictionary* treats the matter smugly: "Careful writers do not use *contact* as a verb.

Instead of *contacting someone,* they *call,* or *write,* or *visit* him."
This last sentence precisely illustrates the semantic economies that
the functional shift of the noun *contact* to verb has made possible,
and so explains the probable reason for the ultimate success of
contact as an American English verb, while at the same time it
illustrates clearly how silly it is for a dictionary to give oversimple,
inaccurate advice on usage. *Oxford American Dictionary'*s note
serves just about the same purpose as does the comment of the
proud mother of the rookie soldier on parade: "Look, everybody's
out of step but Willie!"

It's equally important to see that *Ninth New Collegiate'*s note is
more valuable on this matter of usage than is *American Heritage
II's.* The *Ninth'*s note explains and evaluates the issue and its
defenders, instead of suggesting somehow, as does *American Heritage II,* or asserting flatly, as does *Oxford American,* that *nice*
people don't use *contact* as a verb, when in fact it's perfectly clear
that a very great many of them—in fact *most* of them—*do. Ninth
New Collegiate'*s note puts the reader on notice that there are still a
few out there who continue to object to written and therefore
possibly even to formal spoken use of *contact* as a verb. But with its
ironic "defenders of the language," the *Ninth* also suggests how
seriously we probably ought to take such people: not very. From
that note, the dictionary user can decide whether to push on and
ignore those few objectors, or deliberately to shock them, or, so
long as it costs him nothing and doesn't make him sound silly and
stuffy to others he hopes also to please, to find a circumlocution
and try to please the objectors too. The interesting thing is that the
entrenched elderly and their allies have managed to continue and
extend the fuss over *contact* far beyond the time when it had
become widely and acceptably used by nearly everyone else.

I feel more secure today than I would have in 1966, however,
when I say that *contact* as a verb will triumph completely because
the entrenched elderly have not succeeded in making it a shibboleth in the eyes and ears of the rest of the generations. It is almost
certainly not the kind of shibboleth that will last beyond the
American Heritage usage panel's generation. One cannot speak so
of every usage item today (which is why we must look carefully at
details), but we can be sure of this one so long as the item does not

become shibboleth, touchstone, and cause célèbre, all rolled into one, as did the double negative.

The double negative is worth remembering. We have always had the double negative in English, and until the eighteenth century it was perfectly acceptable from the lips and pens of kings and playwrights alike. (In *As You Like It* Celia says, "I cannot goe no further." 2.4.10) But then it was driven from respectable use by the social strength of those who decided to apply the logic of artificial languages such as mathematics to our natural language. On the argument that two negatives make a positive (which in mathematics of course they do), they based their effort to push the double negative out of acceptable use. Putting mind over manners is chancy and difficult; usually it won't work at all, or if it works at first, the victory won't last. But these eighteenth-century Englishmen had so much social power and worked so hard that they succeeded. Their success probably had little to do with logic; they were successful because they were powerful. In English, a natural language, two negatives don't make a positive: *Don't never do that again!* is still and always has been emphatically negative. So are *I didn't say nothing to him* and *Haven't you got no money?* The double negative simply went out of style like codpieces and powdered wigs; the arbiters of manners and taste said it wasn't done. So the double negative became and remains bad manners. It still works perfectly, but it marks the inadvertent user as vulgar, so it is no more acceptable as Standard English than a sweatshirt at an embassy tea. The completeness of the triumph can be measured by this fact: Standard speakers often use the double negative jocularly; you can do that only if *everybody* knows it's wrong.

What happened to the double negative could of course happen to any other usage item; *contact* too could be made an all-powerful sign of the vulgarity of its users, if everyone who is anyone were agreed that that's what it is. But in the case of *contact* as a verb, I think the bird has flown. Too few of those who are anyone still reprehend it, and those last few are rapidly dying off. They have not succeeded in passing this one down to succeeding generations. If you have any doubt, just contact your latest lexicographer.

A usage item of a different sort and with a somewhat different history and prognosis is the use of *like* as a conjunction (*The cookies look like they're done*). This one too is in large part a contest between the generations. *Like* has been used as a conjunction for many centuries; *OED*'s citations reflect a number of such uses from the late Middle Ages, and reputable authors from every century since have used *like* as a conjunction to mean *as if, as though*, or *as*. But in the nineteenth century some grammarians began to object to the use of *like* in some functions, perhaps because the word was functionally so versatile. Today we use it as a noun (*We'll never see his like again*), an adjective (*I'm of like mind*), an adverb (*It feels more like eighty degrees* or *He was stringy-like in build*) a verb (*I like ice cream*), an auxiliary in the vulgate (*I like to died*), and as a much-deplored interjection of the sort that peppers the talk of so many of the unpliant young these days (*Like, I was, like, already feeling, like, sick, like, before the accident, like*). And since it also appears regularly, if not always happily, as a conjunction (*I feel like I'm going to be sick*), we can conclude that the only part of speech *like* isn't is a pronoun.

That functional versatility may have caused some nineteenth-century compulsives to start trying to limit its functions. After considerable vigorous discussion, they decided that *like* was certainly a preposition, and that therefore it could not also be a conjunction. Curiously enough, not only has it long been both preposition and conjunction, it is by no means the only one of our function words that appears regularly as both preposition and conjunction. *But* is both coordinating conjunction (*I spoke, but he didn't*) and preposition (*Everyone's here but Shirley*). And *since, after*, and *before* all lead double lives as prepositions (*He's been here since nightfall. She arrived after sunset. They saw it before dark.*) and as subordinating conjunctions (*Since he came, we've had no sleep. I'll see them after I get lunch. Call her before you go.*). Nor do these double lives mean that one function must play Mr. Hyde to the other's Dr. Jekyll; both are perfectly respectable. It's a fact of life that natural languages differ in this respect from artificial ones: the symbols used in natural languages frequently have multiple meanings and perform multiple functions, whereas ideally, in an artificial language each symbol with have only one meaning and only one function.

At any rate, the nineteenth century did a double-negative-style job on *like* as a conjunction. While the enforcers didn't succeed in

driving it out of the language, they did succeed in making its use be
considered bad manners. Proper people were said not to use *like* as
a conjunction, so if you were or wished to be thought a proper
person, neither did you. But in fact, *like* as conjunction has always
kept very close to the standard language.

The curious thing about the last twenty years of *like*'s history as a
conjunction is that until quite recently movement in either direction had been very slow; *like* had hung around as colloquial at best
or maybe slightly worse in some usages for some time. ACD (1958)
labeled the "as if" meaning *colloquial,* and ACD's most modern
descendant, *Random House Revised* (1980), calls both that sense
and the sense of "in the same way as; just as, as: *It happened like you
said it would,*" "*Non-standard.*" On the evidence of those two
labels, *like* would appear to have lost a bit of ground between the
early 1960s and today, or at least one might infer from the *Nonstandard* label that today *Random House Revised* does not believe it
is any kind of Standard English, not even informal or colloquial.

The old Funk and Wagnalls *College Standard Dictionary* of
1956 is even more rigorous: it has no entry at all for *like* as a
conjunction. To its editors, the usage should not exist, apparently,
and its absence from their book should make it plain that that use is
not for us, either. But Funk and Wagnalls' more recent college
dictionary, *SCD* (1963), calls the "As if" sense "*Informal.*" Both
New World (1960) and *New World II* (1980) label both senses of *like*
as conjunction "colloquial," with no change over the twenty-year
period.

Yet the use does seem to have gained some ground, particularly
in speech and in use in some less formal levels of the written
language. The Merriam and American Heritage dictionaries illustrate the changes I see.

Prior to *Webster III*'s publication in 1961, the latest Merriam
collegiate dictionary, the *Sixth New Collegiate* (1949–60), gave
an illustration from Keats using *like* as a conjunction, but then
added the following usage note: "*Like* introducing a clause, either
a complete clause or one in which the predicate is to be supplied
from the context, is common in popular usage, but in the work of
careful writers is usually replaced by *as.*" Its example of a use with
predicate supplied from context, "He took to figures like a duck to
water," was a sort of hedge and a far cry from the egregious

examples that have tormented us for the past twenty years, such as these: "Winston tastes good, like a cigarette should." Or, "I feel like I'm falling in love." Whether that issue was being skirted or was instead being viewed as completely beyond the pale is unclear from the 1960 Merriam note.

In 1961 *Webster III* listed many examples of *like* as a conjunction, and of all senses, gave only one a label: *archaic*. The hitherto questionable usage, as in these citations from *Webster III*'s entry, was clearly illustrated and clearly taken to be Standard English: "It looks~he will get the job," and "The violin now sounds~an old masterpiece should." The 1963 *Seventh New Collegiate* of course had a much briefer entry for *like*, conjunction, but it too faced the problem squarely and gave the following example without any usage label or note: "looked~he was scared." In the Merriam view, by 1961 *like* as conjunction was standard.

American Heritage (1969) pulled no punches. It did *not* agree that *like* as a conjunction had arrived. Both senses of the conjunction were labeled *Nonstandard*, and the entry was followed by a long, detailed usage note with quotations (this, remember, was 1969 and almost a decade later than Merriam's first decision to label it no longer):

Like, as a conjunction, is not appropriate to formal usage, especially written usage, except in certain constructions noted below. On other levels it occurs frequently, especially in casual speech and in writing representing speech. In formal usage the conjunctive *like* is most acceptable when it introduces an elliptical clause in which the verb is not expressed: *He took to politics like a fish to water. The dress looked like new.* Both examples, which are acceptable on a formal level to 76 per cent of the Usage Panel, employ such elliptical, or shortened, expressions following *like*. If they were recast to include full clauses containing verbs, *like* would preferably be replaced, in formal usage, by *as, as if,* or *as though: took to politics as a fish takes to water; dress looked as if it were new.* The examples that follow illustrate the difference. All employ *like* to introduce full clauses containing verbs; all are termed unacceptable by more than 75 percent of the Usage Panel, and in every case a more desirable construction is indicated: *He manipulates an audience like* (preferably as) *a virtuoso commands a musical instrument. The engine responds now like* (preferably *as*) *good machinery should. It looks like* (preferably *as if*) *they will be finished earlier than usual. He had no authority, but he always acted like* (preferably *as if*) *he did.* The restriction on *like* as a conjunction does not affect its other uses. Fear of misusing *like* often causes writers to use *as* in its place in constructions where *like* is not only acceptable but clearly called for. It is always used acceptably when it functions prepositionally, followed by a noun or pronoun as object: *works like a charm; sings like an angel; looking for a girl like me* (not *I*); *spoke like one who had authority* (but not *like he had authority*). Used prepositionally, *like* indicates comparison; in modern usage *as*, in place of *like*, would imply the assumption of another role: *He behaved like* (not *as*) *a child. She treated him like* (not *as*) *a fool. John, like* (not *as*) *his grandfather earlier, chose to ignore politics.*

The advice was pretty clear: don't use *like* to introduce full clauses. Also clear was the impact on usage caused by constant admonition that *like* is not a proper conjunction. People have been warned so often that fear of getting it wrong has caused them to overcorrect, so they shun *like* where it could properly serve and frequently use *as* where prepositional *like* is expected. It's the same sort of confusion we've caused with all the drill on case in pronouns, as we'll see in a later chapter.

By 1982 *American Heritage II* clearly senses more change, and its editors also level with us a bit more about the history of this usage problem. They assign no usage label whatsoever, but in a revised usage note tell us what "Prudence requires," and what the usage panel's majority will accept:

Like has been used as a conjunction since Shakespeare's time by the best writers. But the usage has been so vehemently attacked by purists in recent times that the sensible writer will avoid it lest his readers pay more attention to his words than their content. Prudence requires *The engine responds as* (not *like*) *it should.* Constructions like *looks like, sounds like,* and *tastes like* are less likely to offend, but *as if* is better used in formal style: *It looks as if* (not *like*) *there will be another drought.* There can be no objection to the use of *like* as a conjunction when the following verb is not expressed: *He took to politics like a duck to water.* This usage is acceptable to a majority of the Usage Panel.

So, in *American Heritage II*'s opinion, more uses of conjunctive *like* are acceptable today, even though Prudence (not always affable, but usually a sensible editor) requires that we recognize that others are still unacceptable. Note, however, that anyone who had never before encountered the exceptions to the general taboo against *like* as conjunction might find the various special situations somewhat daunting to master. The temptation would almost certainly be to excise *like* from all difficult or doubtful positions and perhaps inadvertently from others.

The latest Merriam college dictionary, the *Ninth New Colle-*

giate (1983) covers much similar ground in its entry, which still
carries no usage label, just as the 1961 and 1963 Merriam books did
not, but it now has a usage note that provides some history and a
good deal more candor than earlier Merriam books had offered
(Keats and Norman Mailer provide the illustrative citations):

The use of *like* as a conjunction may have had its origin in a compound
conjunction *like as*, which is attested as early as the 14th century and
continued into the 19th. But *like* without *as* is also attested as early as the
14th century, and *like* went on being used alone without comment until
sometime in the mid-19th century. It has been stigmatized since then, but
at first not on the grounds that it could not be used as a conjunction; 19th
century grammarians were wrangling over whether *like* should be called a
preposition or not. There is no doubt that after 450 years of use, *like* is
firmly established as a conjunction. It has been used by many prestigious
literary figures of the past, though perhaps not in their most elevated works;
in modern use it may be found in literature, journalism, and scholarly
writing. While the present objection to it is perhaps more heated than
rational, someone writing formal prose may want to use *as* instead.

What is perhaps most fascinating here is the pretty clear implication that *like* as a conjunction, even though it has never wavered in
the vulgate, may have come very close to becoming that kind of
shibboleth we discussed above and illustrated with the double
negative. Yet today it is much used outside the vulgate; Standard
English speakers both speak and write it in all but the most formal
situations—and some of them use it even there. What does the
future hold?

I note first my own practice, falling as I am more and more into
the elderly age-group, if not always into its opinions. I never
use—nor have I ever as an adult used—*like* as a conjunction even
conversationally, except with quotes around it, as a consciously
waggish locution that I use only when I think my hearers will
realize that my use of it is deliberate. Moreover I still notice it in the
speech or writing of those around me, although I rarely correct
anyone who doesn't ask for correction, except in the writing my
students do for publication: there, obviously, Prudence is the guide
to follow. In any event, I conclude both from the advice of the
lexicographers and from the evidence of my own observations and
of my own practice that there may well be at least a full generation
of further wear and tear required before Prudence can in good
conscience give over on this one.

But I note too that there have been changes in the past twenty years, changes both in the distribution of the usage itself and in the dictionaries' approach to giving advice about it. It was a busy twenty years for *like* as a conjunction, and I doubt that we've yet heard the end of the wrangling. It looks like it'll be necessary for at least one more generation to die off—mine. No, I simply can't let it stand; I've got to write *as though* or *as if*. You may do as you like, but for my Standard-speaking contemporaries and me, *like* as a conjunction still doesn't sound right. Using *like* as a conjunction or not using it is truly a generational thing. And it illustrates nicely the fact that the differences between the generations are very large forces indeed in the linguistic change and variation we call usage.

CHAPTER 10

The Battle of the Sexes

Men and women have been at war for a long, long time, and the issues have nearly always been variations of this question: Which of us shall rule the other? Henpecked medieval Noah couldn't get his scold of a wife to board the Ark. Lady Macbeth insisted that she was a better man than Macbeth. Lysistrata and her friends withheld their favors until they got their way. Molière's bluestockinged ladies won the day with wit. And the Wife of Bath outtalked and outfoxed her husbands till she won the *gouvernaunce*. All these female winners had one thing at least in common: sharp tongues. All could use the language as bludgeon or as rapier, and when they won their battles, they almost always used their mastery of the language as a most potent weapon. It seemed that women could triumph in the battle of the sexes only because they were smarter and quicker and could talk faster and better than their male opponents; if women couldn't overcome by harangue or guile or wit, then they were not likely to win at all. Without those weapons, there would be no real contest, for the rules of the game were stacked against them, as in her prologue the Wife of Bath reminded all pilgrims. Ever since Eve, men seem to have had the physical strength, the financial resource, the legal right, the theological sanction, and the political upper hand. And ever since Eve as medieval Christianity pictured her, men seem to have had a clear mandate to rule these fractious temptresses. *"In principio,"* says that master mistranslator Chantecleer to his Dame Pertelote, *"Mulier est hominis confusio."**

If the odds really are so heavily rigged against them before the

---

*The rooster translates it for his lady love: "Woman is man's joy and all his bliss"; actually, *"In principio"* is a tag from John 1:1, which for medieval Christians meant "in the beginning," and so, almost magically, "It's the gospel truth." The rest of the Latin, of course, is really "woman is man's ruination."

contest even begins, it's little wonder that women rail against the system, even as they sharpen whatever weapons they have at hand. Their spokesmen (-persons? -women?) insist that women must fight twice as hard and twice as skillfully as men just to hold their own.

According to some of the feminists of the past twenty years, one major source of the deck-stacking and odds-rigging that English-speaking females face is the English language itself. The very language, they argue, is laid out so as to favor men. These feminists claim that English grammar—its morphology and its syntax—and the English vocabulary—its words and their meanings—are slanted and loaded in ways that foster feelings of inferiority in women and so assist men in their domination of women. Thanks particularly to American feminists of the 1970s and early 1980s, the past twenty years have seen both the renewal of some old arguments on this score and the introduction of some new ones.

Some of these ideas and arguments about the way the language may be rigged in favor of men had been suggested earlier by a variety of people. In a very good assessment of the situation in 1972, Mary Ritchie Key remarks,

As far as the languages of Western societies are concerned, comments on sex differences have crept into writings and studies on other subjects by authors and scholars such as Mulcaster, 1582, Swift, 1735, Lord Chesterfield, 1754, Greenough and Kittredge, 1901 [and] Jespersen, 1921. (281)

But the modern feminist movement, which was just beginning to hit its stride in the early 1970s, has stimulated scholars both male and female to reexamine the structure of English for the signs of such prejudicial features as were said to be built into it. Long before all the evidence was in and evaluated (as indeed it still is not), some feminists began to advocate various changes in the language, changes that would either unseat the masculine "mechanisms" and put feminine "devices" in their places or simply remove what seemed unfair. Some of the scholarship that this burst of industry produced was accurate and its conclusions were sensible; some, alas, was precooked and strident, and its findings were silly. But it all had an effect, and by the time I returned to teaching, feminist marks (some of them scars) were clearly on the language, for better or for worse. Some of the changes wrought by this phase of the battle of the sexes are clearly trivial and likely to be short-lived; some have already faded perceptibly. But a few are much more significant, and these are likely to leave the language changed for many years to come.

I interrupt myself here to observe that some readers may already feel temperature and dander rising; holders of every shade of opinion on this subject seem highly susceptible to paranoia and equally quick to spot it in others. Let me be cool and clinical enough to observe that for those who maintain objectivity, this chapter will also illustrate two additional truths about language. They bear on the gender issue, but only indirectly. One shows us almost effortlessly the intensity of the emotions that matters linguistic can evoke: almost any words can be "fightin' words." And the other makes clear that tinkering selectively with the language can sometimes bring about modest change, while attempts at wholesale revision and major surgery usually accomplish little or nothing.

Linguists, interested as they are both in specific languages and in Language with a capital L, have long theorized about the differing linguistic behaviors of male and female. The past decade in particular has seen a good deal of both basic scholarly research on and anecdotal popular description of sexual variation in the social act of using language. (For references to scholarship, see the headnote of this volume's bibliography.) Differences probably exist—phonological, grammatical, semantic, and possibly other sorts too; but a major question about all of them remains as yet unanswered: are these differences matters of genetic variation or of social conditioning (just like any other manners, such as the choice between the curtsy and the bow), or are they the result of conditioning done by the language itself, so that choosing among its grammatical devices and its semantic options forces women into unconscious patterns of speaking and writing that are different from and of less power than those that men use? Or—as seems likely—are all three sources of difference at work?

A crude illustration may make a bit clearer this matter of the conditioning said to be done by the language itself. Old English at one time had a pronoun declension for the *dual* number; that is, it had a set of forms for the singular pronouns, another set for the dual, and still another for the plural. The singular pronouns were used to refer to one person or thing, the dual to two, and the plural to three or more. During the Old English period, the dual pronouns atrophied and disappeared, and English wound up equipped with a pronoun system essentially like that we have today: a group of singular pronouns for reference to one person or thing, and a group of plural pronouns for reference to two or more.

Now, with that in mind, consider for a moment the Sapir-Whorf hypothesis (named for the famous American linguists and anthropologists who developed it). This hypothesis suggests that we each can see the world only as the grammar of our native language permits or forces us to see it. So, if the hypothesis be accurate, we speakers of Modern English see the world and everything in it as either singular or plural. Thus, when it comes time to pick out a pronoun, we'll pick out one that is singular or one that is plural, according to what we have seen. And we'll make *that* choice only; we cannot choose to use a pronoun from a declension that is neither singular nor plural, one that is neutral on the issue of number; our language doesn't have one. The hypothesis suggests that our language won't let us turn off the mechanism for number; it works all the time, so we English speakers have to view the things we perceive as being one or the other, singular or plural. But the Old English speaker, in the days when the dual pronouns were still in use, had a tripartite view of his world; what he saw was bound to be either singular, dual, or plural. And the idea of *plural* was different in those days, conveying a way of organizing reality that we can no longer convey by a simple choice of pronoun. The speaker of Old English had no freedom in the matter: he *had* to think about the world in terms of one, or two, or three or more; his language insisted that his world was organized that way, and, the hypothesis suggests, his language made him think and speak that way about it. He couldn't NOT speak and think that way; his language had conditioned his view of the world.

Tense is another grammatical device that might illustrate the theory that our language makes us think and act the way it dictates. In English, whenever we use a verb, we have to put it in a tense; ordinarily, we can't duck making a choice of present or past or (with auxiliaries) a so-called perfect or future tense. We can't avoid making a statement about time, even when time is of no particular conscious interest to us. We don't have the option of making a statement without it.

So, it might be argued under this hypothesis that our language conditions us to choose a number and a tense every time we make a statement, even if we're not consciously saying anything about either number or time. There is much, much more that might be said about this sort of theorizing, and not all scholars believe that it will ever be anything more than a hypothesis. * What is important to our discussion of recent developments in American English is the fact that a great many feminists have asserted and some have argued that certain features of the English language similarly condition women who speak it to feel inferior or weak or second class, and condition men to feel superior, strong, and first class in comparison to women.

Grammatically, the first issue concerns the only signals Modern English has that distinguish sex or its absence: the third-person singular personal pronouns. *He/she/it* and its other case forms, *his/her/its* and *him/her/it*, plus the special possessive forms used without following nouns (*his/hers/its*), are the only grammatical signs we have left that signal gender. And, as we'll see, those signs are by no means unequivocal.

A bit of history first. Old English had, and a number of modern languages such as French and German still have, something called *grammatical gender*, a set of signals from the forms or endings of words which identify the words as being masculine, feminine, or neuter in gender. The terms describe a set of factors that actually have nothing to do with the sex (or absence of it) of the referent; X-type, Y-type, and Z-type would have been perfectly good names for the three kinds of grammatical gender, and they'd have been less misleading. But tradition has used these terms for centuries, and we're stuck with them today. At any rate, in Old English, for example, one word meaning "woman," *wifmann*, was masculine, another word with the same meaning, *wif*, was neuter, and the word that meant "lady," *hlæfdige*, was feminine. *Sunne*, "sun,"

---

*Should it be *a hypothesis* or *an hypothesis*? Is Smith *a historian* or *an historian*? In speech, it all depends on the way you say it. If the *h* is aspirated clearly, then the *a* is the article, but if, as so often we do in connected discourse, we suppress or drop the *h*, then what we say is *an istorian*. The question for published prose is, how should we figure you're going to read it? My guess is reflected in the text.

was feminine, *mona*, "moon," was masculine, and *tungol*, "star," was neuter. In languages with grammatical gender, neither maleness, femaleness, nor the absence of any sexually distinguishing characteristics has any bearing on whether a noun or pronoun is grammatically masculine, feminine, or neuter. In Old English, grammatical gender was a powerful set of signals, dictating the inflections (endings) on demonstratives and other adjectives, as well as on nouns and pronouns, and controlling the choice of personal pronoun used for reference. But Modern English no longer has grammatical gender.

Instead, Modern English has only what we call *natural gender*, but the actual operation of pronoun reference—the only place we can indicate gender grammatically—is a bit more complicated than that simple statement suggests. *He* (and its other case forms) is masculine, and if we have a noun whose referent is clearly sexually male, we'll use *he*, *his*, or *him* to refer to it, as we do with *father*, *monk*, *gentleman*, and *brother*. Note that *priest* used to be one of these words too, but that it is no longer a role restricted to males. One of my colleagues assures me that his wife is an Episcopal *priest*, not a *priestess*. Here then is another detail to help fill out our picture of change in the language, in this instance caused by a change in the character of the referent, a change involving the battle of the sexes, and within the past twenty years, too.

If our noun is one like *woman*, *mother*, *sister*, *waitress*, or *nun*, we'll use the *she* forms for pronoun reference. But, as has happened to *priest*, we'll find a change in the possible referent of *queen*, which today can also mean an effeminate homosexual male. And if our noun clearly has no sex, like *house*, *sleet*, *yellow*, *music*, or *grassland*, then we'll refer to it with *it* forms.

But those are only the three main generalizations. English also has words whose referents do have a sex (such as *dog*, *cat*, and *baby*), but in which we often can't tell which sex is represented. Again, remember that we're interested only in the singular, because *they*, *their*, *them*, and *theirs*, the plural pronouns, don't have gender, nor do they give any information about sex or the lack of it in the referent; *dogs* is plural, and *they* can be all male, all female, or a mixed group of some of each; *rocks*, however, are without sexual qualities, even though *they* is the proper pronoun for *them*, too. Then, of course, there are nouns like *rooster* or *bull*; with such words we can use either *it* or *he*; choice of the neuter may suggest that we don't know the sex or aren't sure of it, or may indicate that the matter is of no interest: somehow, all cattle are cows for our urban purposes, since milk comes from cartons. And there is a comparable list of words like *hen* and *cow*, each of which can be referred to by either *she* or *it*. Then there are the nouns that can take *any* of the three third-person singular pronouns, *he, she,* or *it*: words like *dog, horse,* and *lion* fit this group, as do *one, other,* and *another* (*Another came in through the door, and they shot him, her, or it*). Next there is a group of words like *team, gang,* and *committee,* which in their singular forms can be referred to with either *it* (neuter) or *they* (no gender). And finally there is the list of words like *somebody, someone, anybody, anyone, everybody, everyone, person,* and *each*; each of these words except *each* can be referred to by *he, she,* or *they,* even though all are apparently singular, and *each,* depending on its use, can be covered by those same three pronouns plus *it* (as in *each of these words*). These lists of pronouns and the kinds of nouns they can refer to can be found in C. Nelson Francis's *The Structure of American English* (250–51), but note that in the twenty-five years or so since he put the list together, two of the words, *priest* and *queen,* and possibly some others whose referents have shifted in the same way, no longer fit Francis's classifications. *Soprano* never did fit, I think; Francis classed it as a word that always called for *she* as pronoun, but in fact it is also used to stand for at least three other referents, one of which is male (the young boy who sings in a choir), one of which may be either male or female (the player of the smallest and highest pitched of the saxophones), and two of which are neuter (that saxophone itself and the musical part itself, as printed or as drummed out on a piano: *This is the soprano*). Pronoun reference is a complicated business, and some recent feminist efforts have changed some referents, particularly as women have taken up what were once considered traditionally male occupations such as priest, lifeguard, or marine.

Also as background we need to remark on the curious use of the feminine pronouns for ships and cars and the like: *She's a beauty* and *Give 'er the gas*. And then there was that historian friend who stopped me several years ago to ask about a public statement of mine in which I had referred to *the University and those who love her.* "How did you come to use *her* to refer to the University?" she asked. It's hard to be certain that referring to the *yacht* as *she* is not in fact one more sexually driven choice from the same old sexist origin, in which the owner-yachtsman uses the same term of endearment about this beloved object as he might use about his wife, his mistress, or his sports car; but my answer to the historian perhaps puts a different sort of "English" on the university as *she*: *alma mater* is an old and I trust benign sexist term. There is at least one thing a man can't be.

But the two issues commanding by far the greatest amount of time, effort, and ink are the use of the masculine singular third-person pronoun as the generic pronoun in sentences like *Everybody took off his coat*, and the use of compounds containing the word *man*. Let's look at the grammatical issue first.

The masculine singular pronoun has been specified by Standard English for many years as the form to use with all those indefinite pronouns listed above, in utterances and especially in written sentences like these: *Somebody forgot his calculator,* or *Each is to purchase his own dictionary,* or *Everybody took off his coat.* To insist on the exclusive use of the masculine as the generic is, say feminists, unfairly to load the language to make males seem more important than females. If the Sapir-Whorf hypothesis is accurate, we must see the world as the grammar of our language organizes it for us. If that be true, then the use of masculine pronouns for generic male, female, or sexually mixed or unclassified referents could well appear to exclude women. If the generic singular pronoun is always masculine, then the language discriminates against women.

So feminists have proposed several programs for modifying or changing the language in order to undo the subliminal damage they believe this grammatical feature is doing. Some have argued that the thing to do is simply to substitute the feminine pronoun for the masculine. Make the feminine pronoun the generic instead, and use *Everybody took off her coat* on all occasions, whether the group referent is all female, mixed, or all male. The argument is that in the last instance, the *her* would be just as fair to males as the *his* is for reference to an all-female group or, for that matter, to a mixed group. One could put up a counterargument, I suppose, to the effect that replacing one bias with another bias is not really to improve the situation. But there remains the question of whether that "bias" of the masculine generic is in fact a real bias. Don't their mixed referents affect the "sexuality" of the generic pronouns at all?

There are at least two other problems with this proposed solution to the question of the masculine generic; both have been brought forcibly to my attention since my return to teaching. The first problem is that to most people the feminine pronouns sound very odd as generics. Consider the following passage, which comes from an excellent essay on children's acquisition of language. Even female students of mine complained that the essayist's programmatic use of feminine generic pronouns in sentences like these and others throughout the essay was "distracting and silly."

While a child is still babbling, adults may address long, complex sentences to her, but as soon as she begins to utter meaningful, identifiable words they almost invariably speak to her in very simple sentences. Over the next few years of the child's language development the speech addressed to her by her caretakers may well be describable by a grammar only six months in advance of her own. (Moskowitz, 168)

Distracting it certainly is at first, and of course that may be one of its purposes, given the general idea of "consciousness-raising" that has been one of the goals of feminists. It does indeed serve the purpose of getting the reader's attention, just as any loud break with conventional manners will do. The difficulty is that it gets the reader's attention at the expense of his grasp of the text.

My guess is that those who have adopted this substitution for the generic masculine pronoun eventually hope either entirely to supplant the masculine pronoun with the feminine, or to gain equal use for a feminine generic, with feminists using the latter pronoun and sexists the former. I doubt that either of these things will come to pass. The first will almost certainly not work, for at least two reasons that together seem to me quite persuasive.

There will almost certainly continue to be great resistance to the substitution simply because we have so much invested in past prose that uses the masculine as the generic. Even though the teaching and other efforts at propagation and continuation of the masculine generic have not been particularly successful over the years (it is in

fact losing ground, though not much of it to the feminine pronoun), society counts the pattern as "good manners," even if it
can't or won't always practice them.

I've read a number of popular articles aimed at a general audience by feminists attempting to persuade about feminist topics, and
I'd guess that this substitution succeeds in persuading readers that
the language actually may be conditioning its users unconsciously
to exclude or undervalue the female. But just as important, I think,
is the fact that the use of the feminine generic is distracting in any
writing that, like the Moskowitz essay quoted above, has its main
argument on an entirely different, nonfeminist subject. Moskowitz
and others of her opinion hope, I'm sure, that readers like my
students and me will eventually get used to the practice, and that
after a while it won't be an irritant constantly interfering between
the main purpose of her writing and us. If there were a universal
change, of course we *would* get used to it in time. But such a
change seems unlikely because most English prose, past and present, doesn't use the feminine generic, and besides, those of us who
have succeeded in mastering the use of the masculine, at least for
our formal prose, will not lightly give up something so hard won.
I'll return to this point a bit later on.

The second reason is the clincher, however: if any supplanting is
done, it won't be the feminine generic that supplants; it'll be the
plural generic, as in *Everybody took off their coats(s)*; the process
has long been complete in the common language, and in the
standard is probably far enough along that it may need only to bury
a generation or two more and thus drive the singular generic—*any*
singular generic—out of its last stronghold, the formal language,
especially the formal *written* language. I'll say more of this later,
too.

A second programmatic approach proposed as a way of undoing
this possibly unfair bit of English grammar is simply to urge
everyone to use *both* the masculine and feminine on all occasions
where the generic might have been used (*Everybody took off his or
her coat*). In legal prose such as statutes, by-laws, contracts, and the
like, this step has already taken place in the effort to achieve
completeness and precision, even at the expense of clarity and
grace. Other elephantine efforts along similar lines have been

proposals to use coinages such as (s)*he* or *s/he* as a hermaphroditic all-purpose pronoun, or the ugly-looking and uglier-sounding *him/her* construction (to be read aloud as "him slash her," I presume—in my opinion a locution hard to match for all-round bloodiness). But outside the realm of legalistic prose trying to achieve a precision that will always seem to elude its writers, most of the rest of us, and certainly writers who have any ear for euphony, will avoid these pasteups.

The efforts at replacing the masculine generic pronoun, then, are unquestionably the main *grammatical* change that feminism has tried to bring about. It has had two results, neither of them precisely what the feminists had sought, I suspect, but perhaps changes they might think better than nothing. The first is the change mentioned briefly above. Efforts to suppress the masculine-singular generic pronoun have not succeeded in supplanting it with feminine pronouns or with either-or pairs in Noah's ark style, or with any of the made-up candidates. What these efforts *have* done is to give great new impetus to the replacement of the generic masculine singular with the plural. *Everybody took off their coats* has been in the vulgate for generations, but for a long while Miss Dove and Sister Mary Catherine managed to keep it penned up there, at least as far as formal standards for classroom recitation and themes were concerned. But of course in the real world of conversation and memos and other informal writing, the *Everybody . . . their* construction is now almost universal, particularly when what they're going to take off is the plural *coats*, not the singular *coat*. Long, long before feminists began their campaign to do in the masculine generic, usage was well on its way to supplanting it with the plural *their*.

Of course the issue for our schoolteachers was never the question of gender; it was the number of the *Everybody* (singular), the antecedent of the pronoun *their* (plural!). In 1974 the late Robert C. Pooley summed up the situation nicely in his list of "usages which lie outside standard English and are therefore to be avoided" (207). In that list of what must be taught was item number 20: "Proper agreement in number with antecedent pronouns *one* and *anyone, each, no one, either, neither.* With *everybody, everyone, somebody, someone,* and *none* some tolerance of number has long been acceptable, particularly in informal contexts" (208).

So it's clear that the stage was set for this solution to the problem with the generic masculine singular pronoun. Unquestionably, in the last ten years or so, the feminists' campaign has speeded the progress (and probably ensured the ultimate victory) of the plural generic pronoun. And except for rigorous editors and Standard English speakers and writers of my tottering generation (I'd be willing to wager that *American Heritage*'s usage panel would not accept *Everybody put on their coats* in formal writing), this is what most people are using—some on policy, in support of the feminists' goal, but most simply because this once-colloquial usage has continued to win acceptance in more and more spoken and written contexts.

But there's another result that the battle of the sexes' skirmish over the masculine generic pronoun has brought about, and in the long run it could be much more important in that it could cause a whole range of changes in the way American English works. The result is harder to spot, perhaps, but it is clearly there and working. You can read it in the advice of all textbook houses and editors to their authors, and it's there in the advice of readers to writers whose prose may be scrutinized by those who believe with some feminists that the English language is unfair. This result is simply the deliberate and systematic avoidance of the singular in nouns and pronouns of any semantically sexual content. The Prentice-Hall College Division's *Guidelines on Sexism*, a leaflet dated 3/79, is typical; it informs its authors and editors that this sentence is biased: "The typical child does his homework right after school," and that it can be recast in unbiased form thus: "Most children do their homework right after school" (7).

The point is interesting, as is the entire pamphlet. Sometimes the rewritten sentences are improvements; sometimes they are not. Frequently the "unbiased" rewrite is a cumbersome passive voice construction, which of course permits all sorts of things to be done, without anyone actually doing them. It is early days still, I suspect, to conclude that the actual use of the singular will diminish as a result of all this concern over fairness in English grammar.

But a very instructive example is the following, from a pamphlet published by Wesley Theological Seminary, Washington, D.C., entitled *The Use of Inclusive Language in the Worship of the Church*:

As always, care should be taken to avoid clumsiness that calls attention to itself. While personal pronouns may sometimes be eliminated by repeating the use of a non-sexist noun, often a less-obtrusive revision is attained by using the passive voice and relative pronouns. The intensive pronoun can often be avoided through the use of other words, and neologisms can also be circumvented. For example:

EXCLUSIVE
The Holy Spirit in his graciousness makes us a new people. God himself works in us, transforming us according to his will.

INCLUSIVE BUT CLUMSY
The Holy Spirit in the Spirit's graciousness makes us a new people. Godself works in us, transforming us according to God's will.

PREFERABLE
We are made a new people through the graciousness of the Holy Spirit. It is indeed God who works within us, transforming us according to the divine will. (Stookey, 8)

The "Preferable" passage is vague, passive, and 36 percent wordier than the "Exclusive" version. It may be "Inclusive," and that may make it good worship, but in my judgment it's not good prose.

In the final chapter I'll point out that the language we have is the language we need; it's a reflection of the values we hold, the values we want to express. Therefore it is quite safe to assure ourselves that when we stop *being* sexist, the language will automatically modify itself in such a way as not to be sexist either, if indeed it now is. Recasting sentences, as Prentice-Hall's booklet does, can alert us to some tacit assumptions on this or other values we may hold without consciously realizing it. That may be an important exercise in self-awareness. But there is real question whether approaching the solution of the problem by treating its grammatical symptoms is likely to be very successful. And if, because the referent has changed, *officer* and *priest* are now either masculine or feminine, then once more depending on context, why isn't generic *his* either masculine or feminine as well? In this instance, I think that's what *generic* means: "refers to *either* kind."

The other major effect the feminist movement has had on the language is on the vocabulary. Under a heading *"Human, Not Man: Describing the World,"* the Prentice-Hall booklet says:

One way to establish an unbiased tone that treats people as individuals who share universal human characteristics and traits is to avoid the use of the word *man* to mean all people and the use of *-man* words in general. If such words must be used, they should be accompanied by an explanation or be set in a context that clearly does not exclude women. (7)

Probably there is little need to drag out all the earnest efforts that have been made to do away with terms like *chairman* and *freshmen*. We're all capable of endless silliness, and both sides in this quarrel have performed in exemplary fashion to prove it. *Chairperson* has caught on, although *freshpersons* has not. And we'll not soon excise the *-man-* syllable from words like *penmanship*. What I think is important is that we keep a few principles in mind. First, our vocabulary is constantly in a state of change, and we'll find new words or new meanings for old words if and when the referents change. As with *priestess*, so with *policewoman*; we've gone to the more nearly generic term because we need it; when they were few and rarely seen, *policewoman* and *woman doctor* were inevitable terms, like *male nurse*. Now *doctor, lawyer, merchant,* and *thief* can take either *he* or *she* pronouns, and so it's not surprising to see the more generic term *officer* replace the sex-linked names for the cops. When the force is mixed, *policemen* and *policewomen* are too cumbersome to deal with; *police officers* wins the day.

It's interesting to trace some of the older terms for females in traditionally male roles: *aviatrix* went out as an archaism about the time Amelia Earhart disappeared, but *waiter* and *waitress* both still get equal play, and no really useful sexless generic seems to have appeared: it's either "Waitress!," "Waiter!," or "Hey, you!" (and they won't come anyway). My wife is an *actress*, but when she directs plays, she's a *director*. Yet I note that when she refers to the members of the all-female troup she directs in children's plays, she speaks of them as the *actors*. Curiously, it is almost always the masculine (*actor, priest, shepherd*) term that feminists are eager to have be the standard generic. Maybe *his* isn't all bad, after all. The truth is that it's what you think the word stands for that makes all the difference.

A second principle to keep in mind is that our constant manufacture of euphemisms, to make our world look better than it is, usually succeeds only in making us look foolish. The Prentice-Hall pamphlet urges that its authors avoid the biased term *housewife* and choose instead one of these: *homemaker, consumer*. The first is a silly euphemism, and the second means something quite different. So rather than extend this discussion needlessly, I would simply counsel restraint. H. L. Mencken on euphemism is wonderful, salutary reading (1980 ed., 339ff.); he reminds us of the folly of which we are almost endlessly capable when we try to improve our world by changing its names, not its referents.

Man is a compounding syllable far too deeply engrained in the fiber of our lexicon to be rooted out easily, nor, in my view, should it be. The chief generalization to keep in mind when contemplating action along such lines is this: you can occasionally tinker with a word or two, and you may be able to drive a handful of -*man* compounds underground, but sweeping changes such as an academy of feminist language experts might propose simply will not work. And English in particular, both the American and British varieties, has always steadfastly resisted the idea of an academy, as both Jonathan Swift and Noah Webster learned the hard way.

The main truth that came home to me as I ended my twenty-year nap is that the feminist movement has indeed had an effect on American English, and that some of the changes may last. It may well be, however, that the shifts in the vocabulary will amount in the end to a handful of words blacklisted and some dozens of others changed in meaning simply because their referents have changed to include females. The really significant effect may be the hardest of all to measure: the attempt to avoid unconscious sexism by avoiding use of the singular nouns and pronouns where possible. Should any part of that succeed, English syntax could in future look quite different indeed. These things do not happen overnight, but I'm a bit worried at the thought that something might stimulate even greater use of the passive voice than already afflicts the language. Yet we should take comfort in the knowledge that one rarely changes the language by direct attack on it; if the values change, the language will change.

Oh yes, and one more thing: the question of whether a language is or is not fair and unbiased in and of itself. The devices a language uses to signal its grammatical meanings evolve in very complicated ways, so by the time a generic masculine singular evolves, it may be difficult to prove that it is in fact sex-linked in that use any more than grammatical gender was itself sex-linked. But it is clear that efforts to produce a new version of the English language, specially gelded to be fair to any group, is a time-consuming project at best, primarily because to approach the process from that end is probably quite fruitless. When the speakers of the language hold fair values, the language—grammar, lexicon, and all—will reflect them exactly. On certain kinds of sexism, we may find an occasional specific taboo effective. But my guess is that for now, a slower process of change is under way, and that it will in the end do what needs to be done. Trying to work much faster will probably be a waste of time and effort.

CHAPTER 11

The Readiest Measure of Virtue: Spelling

When other people's spelling goes awry, most of us notice at once; my collection of diverting inadvertences began to grow almost as soon as I returned to the classroom. Our eyes are usually pretty quick to spot flaws in others; it's easy to see the other chap's egg stain on the tie, the shoe untied, or the fly not zipped. Misspelled words are like that; we can see them in what others write much more readily than we can find them in what we ourselves have just written.

Every teacher knows what can happen to his own spelling once he devotes himself to student papers. A year of grading them can turn an excellent speller into a basket case. One interesting side effect of my leaving teaching for an extended period was that eventually I recovered my abilities as a speller. I am what is usually called a "visual" speller: I know no rules, and I use almost no mnemonic devices; the visual image of the word correctly spelled is usually all I need (and what I must have). Some people call what I and many other good spellers have "a proofreader's eye"; when we look at a printed page, most misspellings will usually jump to our attention even before we've read the page. Misspelled words just don't *look* right to us. When we correct a misspelled word, we may have to write out several variant possibilities until we find the correct one, the one that looks right.

The curse of that blessing for the teacher, of course, is that his image of the word spelled correctly gets weak and distorted when over the years he keeps seeing it on student papers, spelled wrong almost as often as he sees it spelled right. Finally he is reduced to rubble: he can no longer rely on his visual images of words, and he can no longer spell words that once he spelled automatically. When I left teaching in 1966 I had reached the point where I regularly had to look up dozens of words I had once been able to spell without thinking: was it *aberant* or *abberant* or *aberrant* or *abberrant*? And should it end -*ant* or -*ent*?* At any rate, after a few years away from teaching I began to recover my spelling, and I was almost completely healed by the time I returned to the classroom and the student essay. Alas, it took less than a semester to confound my confusion once more, and today I'm back to looking up word after word, my students having once more filled me full of wrong images and doubt.

But what of spelling in general? Is American English spelling any different today than it was twenty years ago? Many years before that, while I was a graduate student at the University of Michigan, the late Albert H. Marckwardt, one of my teachers, did a survey of various kinds of problems found in student writing, among them student spelling errors. He found that the most frequent errors involved

a. Words that contain unstressed vowels: is it *seperate* or *separate*? *indispensible* or *indispensable*?

b. Metathesis, the name we give that wrong ordering of cart and horse that makes us write *calvary* for *cavalry*.

c. Problems that arise when we add derivative suffixes, as in *arguement* and *desireable*.

d. problems in handling unstressed *i*, as in *efficent*.

The same problems Marckwardt found, along with other familiar ones such as the typographical transpositions and omissions I regularly make when I type *studnet* for *student* and *pubic* for *public*, were still bedeviling my students when I left them in 1966, and it's no surprise to find that not much has changed today: the same errors still call for the teacher's red ink.

We probably know a bit more today about some of the various causes of spelling difficulties; we know that not all who spell badly do so for the same reasons. We know, for example, that a wholly phonetic speller (there aren't many of them, but I've met one or two since my return) gets insufficient help from visual images of words, and therefore finds it difficult to use an ordinary dictionary: he'll keep looking for *phrenology* under *f*. In teaching some poor

---

Aberrant is right. If you study these four variants for a minute or two you can thoroughly confuse yourself, even if you know how the word is spelled.

spellers, oftentimes (we know now) some of our traditional methods do little more than stimulate guilt feelings. Last year one of my seniors gave me a paper with the word *mnemonic* spelled *pnemonic*; it's easy to figure out how she arrived at such an odd spelling for that first consonant sound: she had indeed noticed that *mnemonic* had a very peculiar consonant cluster up front, not the simple *n-* you might expect, so she picked a cluster—the wrong one, by chance—from the list of odd consonant clusters she had in her head. She borrowed from *pneumatic* or *pneumonia*. She knew only that there was something illogical required for *mnemonic*, and she supplied it.

Incidentally, I found on my return that there is now at least one dictionary especially for people who spell mostly phonetically: Peter and Craig Norback's *The Awful Speller's Dictionary*, in which phonetic spellers can find the word *fenomenal* under *f* where they expect it to be, and with it the correct spelling, *phenomenal*. It's a useful book, even if only for a very small number of problem spellers.

Another side of the spelling issue is of even more interest to me, although the attitudinal changes I've been trying to promote in my students since my return seem to have a long road ahead of them. Generally we all quite unfairly use spelling as an easy measure of character and intelligence. Of course spelling has relatively little to do with intelligence, nor is poor spelling an outward and visible sign of inner tendencies toward sin. Thorstein Veblen had it partly right years ago when he observed in his famous *The Theory of the Leisure Class*:

> As felicitous an instance of futile classicism as can well be found, outside of the Far East, is the conventional spelling of the English language. A breach of the proprieties in spelling is extremely annoying and will discredit any writer in the eyes of all persons who are possessed of a developed sense of the true and beautiful. English orthography satisfies all the requirements of the canons of reputability under the law of conspicuous waste. It is archaic, cumbrous, and ineffective; its acquisition consumes much time and effort; failure to acquire it is easy of detection. Therefore it is the first and readiest test of reputability in learning, and conformity to its ritual is indispensable to a blameless scholastic life. (399)

Actually, spelling is mostly a neuromuscular skill in the development of which practice helps, but for which certain innate equipment is the main requirement. Some people can run fast and far; other can swing a golf club skillfully. I can do neither very well, but I can spell—or at least I *used* to be able to, before I returned to teaching. To be able to spell is something to be grateful for, but nothing to boast of as though it were an accomplishment. I tell my freshmen, "The ability to spell is in some respects like physical beauty: it is not given equally to all. But we can all do our best to present ourselves as attractively as possible and to avoid calling attention to our most dismal features. Some of us just have to work harder at it than others. Use your dictionary." And I tell my seniors, before sending them off into the world, "If you're one of those who can't spell, try to marry someone who can. And get a pocket dictionary which you treat like the prosthetic device it must be for you. There's nothing shameful about wearing glasses or hearing aids or dentures. You need a pocket dictionary of spelling words just as much as I need glasses; it's the only way we can live fully and normally without being deprived or otherwise penalized. Your bad spelling is no more shameful than my hyperopia, but we both have to correct our problems if we are not to cripple ourselves for living."

So to use spelling to keep people in their places is wrong, although, as Veblen suggests, we do it all the time. But we shouldn't, and that's my newest goal: to help my students and anyone else who will listen understand what kind of problem spelling really is. We've learned by now not to fear or hate left-handedness; we now design scissors and other tools and furniture for left-handers and think nothing of it. That's the way it ought to be with most bad spellers too: we should help them compensate, but we should not ostracize or punish them further just because they're crippled. If there is any widely held understanding by the general public on this point, however, I have yet to see it. I've got a lot of work to do.

Moreover, people still complain from time to time about the inefficiencies of the English spelling system; they point out how much more efficient are the systems of Italian or Norwegian or some other languages whose spelling systems froze more recently than English, which began its hardening process during the Renaissance and had pretty much completed it by the end of the eighteenth century. Actually, English spelling is not all that bad, especially considering the cosmopolitan lexicon it has assembled. But at any rate, most scholars now agree that wholesale spelling reform won't work in English. Every effort at the sweeping reform of our spelling, like Noah Webster's, Bernard Shaw's, Colonel McCormick's (of the *Chicago Tribune*), and whatever was the proposal of the most recent crusader, is bound to fail. We can tinker and change a word here and there, but to comb the entire language forward and part it orthographically somewhere else is simply not an option open to us. Too much history, too much inertia, too much habit, to say nothing of our own personal investment of time and effort, are locked up in our spelling system. We could not afford full-scale reform financially, intellectually, or emotionally. And we've known it for a long time, even though new reformers keep popping up with wonderful new schemes and fancy new alphabets that won't work either. I find not much change in the matter of spelling reform over the past twenty years, except that skepticism at new reform proposals seems to me a bit more firmly in the saddle. That's a gain.

But I do notice a few developments—just one or two—that come under the heading of tinkering. *Judgment* and *judgement* have both been acceptable spellings in American English for many years, although some dictionaries used to note that the one with the medial *e* was "probably British." But today, even though current college dictionaries usually list the *judgment* spelling first, thus implying that the *e*-less spelling might be encountered a bit more frequently, my experience is that exactly the reverse is the present state of affairs among my students, nearly all of whom now spell it *judgement*. I note this with some rueful amusement, inasmuch as I have taught many of their high school teachers through the years that although either spelling was quite acceptable, more people seemed to be electing *judgment*. Besides, I added (persuasively, I thought), *I* always spell it *judgment*. This failure to win my position may speak to questions of the contest between the generations, of which I've already said much more in another chapter, but at any rate, in this as in many other skirmishes over linguistic manners, I seem to have lost ground—or perhaps even the whole battle— while I was away. This one may be only a local change, of course, and I dare not yet predict a trend. But it *is* a difference.

Here's another, a spelling curiosity that has long been a wholly nonrational one-man crusade of mine: to retain the spelling *adviser* instead of *advisor*. I note wistfully on my return that the forms I sign to approve my students' programs and course changes now label the box for my name "Advisor's Signature." Twenty years ago on this campus, I was a faculty *adviser*, at least whenever I had control of the spelling. There's absolutely nothing wrong with the *-or* spelling, of course; both spellings have been around for a long time, and both the *-er* and *-or* spellings are perfectly acceptable suffixes for adding an agent to a verb; we have many built on each model: *leader, director, publisher, editor, driver, conductor*. Both in Merriam's *Seventh New Collegiate* and in the *Ninth*, *adviser* is listed before *advisor*, though both spellings are clearly quite equally acceptable. When I left teaching, however, I knew I had a battle on my hands if I were to preserve *adviser* here on this campus, although I thought the issue was still in the balance. As I read my way through the piles of university forms and policies today, however, I conclude that on this campus at any rate the issue is no longer in doubt, and I have lost. It will not be long, I fear, before someone will tax me with my quaintly archaic spelling of *adviser*. An antick display.

Another sort of change is illustrated by a new student spelling which I had never encountered until I returned, and which my colleagues and I now see almost every week: *alot*. There's *alot* of *alot* going around, and the interesting thing to me is that many of my most conscientious students have given me papers containing *alot* as the only abnormal spelling. In the history of English there are many instances of our pasting a little word on the front of a big one; typically the telescoping involves a preposition and its object: Old English *on lif* ("on life") becomes *alive*. But we may here have another sort of telescoping. If *inasmuch* and *nevertheless* can stick together, perhaps one day *alot* will too, particularly if a lot of speakers of Standard English decide to write it that way. We'll wait and see. For now, it's no more acceptable than *nitelite*.

For the most part, then, our spelling seems to have remained fairly stable over these twenty years. Oh, in 1973 the Medieval Academy of America at long last dropped its older spelling of *Mediaeval* from the subtitle of its journal, *Speculum*, and in 1980 from the name of the academy itself; and most of the other digraphs (*anaemic, oenology,* and the like) have disappeared from American English in favor of a single vowel, although British English still retains many of the digraphs. We still maintain both spellings of *theater* (with the chiefly British *theatre* used mainly in proper names in this country), but although we are familiar with many other British spellings (the *-our* words, where we usually have *-or,* as in *honor;* the *-ise* and *-isation* spellings, where usually but not always we have *-ize* and *-ization,* as in *civilize* and *civilization;* and the like), we seem not to be adopting any of them in place of our own. Rather, it seems pretty clear that the flow is in the other direction. The British newspapers that I read during a recent trip to London gave me the impression that Londoners, at least, are very familiar with many peculiarly American spellings, and that some are in perfectly respectable use there. One in particular, *jail* for *gaol,* seems to have taken over completely. And I suspect there are others.

One other spelling matter I checked into fairly soon after my return was whether we had adopted any more rigorous party line over whether to separate compound words, hyphenate them, or run them together. We can always be fairly sure that the word or words are true compounds if in speech the stress has moved up to the front syllable, as in *blockhead, ball park, gasworks, gas station, color-blind,* and *gate-crasher.* But, as the examples suggest, we seem to use all three spelling patterns in such a way that it would be difficult to predict the spelled form a new compound might take. There is a kind of generalization that seems to describe large numbers of such locutions, but it is by no means a very powerful generalization, for there are exceptions galore. The generalization says simply that if the compound is brand new, or perhaps still in divided usage as to where the stress falls (take *ice cream,* for example, which we can hear with the stress on either syllable), then it will still be spelled as two words. The next step, says this generalization, is to hyphenate, which will happen as the word becomes fixed in its stress and after it has been for some time in at least the spoken version of the language. Finally, says the generalization, when the compound has been around for a longer time and has appeared more frequently in print, someone is very likely to treat it the way we spell *baseball, basketball, volleyball,* and *football*—both the sports and the balls with which they're played.

But do we keep *soccer ball* as two words, or perhaps as *soccer-ball*, simply because soccer is a relatively less popular game in this country? My guess is that that's not it at all, but rather that the name of the game is the thing: the game is *soccer*, with no mention of a ball, whereas the ball is an integral part of the names of the other four games, just as it is in *pinball*.

Anyway, from looking at my dictionaries and some of the books, journals, and papers I read, I would suggest that there has been no general change in the way we spell compounds, but that indeed a few words individually have moved from two-word to one-word status, with or without passing through a hyphenated stage. New compounds that clearly wasted little time in reaching the single-word stage are *frostbiter* (a small sailboat used for winter class racing; also the sailor who races in it, and sometimes the race itself), *skylounge*, and *skyjack*. *Sailboard* (another kind of sailboat) is also one word, but *growth fund*, *launch window*, and *language laboratory*—like the others above, new since the early 1960s*—are still two words. Words like *sleep-in* and *sit-in*, especially as nouns, seem to hang on to their hyphens, while *skinny-dip*, which most dictionaries used to call slang, is now "*Informal*" in *American Heritage II* and *Random House Revised*, and has no usage label at all in Merriam's *Ninth New Collegiate*. And it seems always to wear its hyphen.

So we may conclude that the generalization, never very powerful and always full of exceptions (*sister-in-law* as a compound has been around for a long time, but shows little sign of closing up into a single word), still is at least of interest. The only really effective way to study the spelling of compound words in English, however, is to examine each on its own merits.

Nonetheless, I have been much diverted by my collections of odd spelling errors, as I suppose we all are. Homophones, those words that sound the same and are spelled differently, still cause a lot of anguish and amusement. A student newspaper is a fine microcosm of the great world of spelling problems: here are a few illustrative samples of homophonic pratfalls:

"Just a few days more than a year ago," wrote the retiring editor,

---

*These and other new words are easily inspected in two specialized dictionaries by Clarence L. Barnhart and others. See the bibliography.

"I took the reigns of The [University of Connecticut] Daily Campus." Regal style; no horsing around.

"This is the first hydroelectric project attempted by DEP," the news story reported, "though there are 26 other state-owned sights under consideration." Beauty spots, I trust.

Here a story quotes a policeman discussing a man who had been holding some hostages: "He threatened their lives. But each time we were able to diffuse it." Which may explain why there's so damned much of this hostage-taking. The *Hartford Courant* recently quoted a politician who said something similar: "I want to diffuse the fears right away that I'd take any part in dumping a Hispanic."

From the sports page comes a fairly standard error, on a par with the *to/too/two* confusion which catches us all: "'They're pitches weren't too good,' Zippel said." Nor was their proofreading.

Another quotation: "A state official . . . said, however, that the group's steering committee 'has widdled it down to 15–20 names.'" Wonderful new verb, I think, illustrating nicely the disappearing "hw" cluster which I still use in saying *whittle*; obviously, this reporter doesn't say it that way.

But it's not fair to pick only on the students. Here's a clipping from an unidentified state newspaper which someone mailed to me. It describes Congressman Stewart McKinney of Fairfield as "a moderate who's survived eight sessions more with guile and constituent service than by towing an ideological line." My image is of the Er-i-e Canal.

And from the *Hartford Courant* comes this headline on a four-column story about the top public relations experts on Capitol Hill: "Magazine Rates Congress' 'Finest Flaks.'" Highest caliber, I suppose they mean. I checked the two words with my students and found fine illustrations of one word drifting toward archaism and obsolescence and another not yet developed much beyond jargon: *flak*, for antiaircraft guns and their bursting shells, is a World War II term borrowed from the Germans (*Fliegerabwehrkanonen*), according to the *Ninth New Collegiate*. It appeared in English about 1938 (a colleague says much earlier), and for the younger generation it's already gone. As soon as the World War II generations die off, the word will be only of historical interest. *Flack*, the P.R. man or press agent, is a 1941 word, according to the *Ninth*, and while the word carries no slang or informal label in *American Heritage II* or the *Ninth*, it's still a fairly specialized term, belonging to the argot of the press and the superstar; many of my students didn't know it.

Spelling isn't much fun, perhaps, but misspelling can be very funny indeed. Certainly on my return I've found business leaders and others worrying about our graduates whom we've failed to teach to spell. I think it's important that we teach those who can learn to do so how to express themselves in decent prose. Spelling is a different matter; its problems haven't changed, but it may well be that a change in our attitudes about how we deal with poor spelling will help more than fulmination, which, over the past twenty years, seems to me not to have contributed anything but increased guilt. We should, I think, be more cheerful about it. To that end, I'll finish this chapter with a few more homophones that got away; these two are from *The Daily Campus* sports page:

The first is about Doug Flutie, who was then finishing up his miracle-working final season as Boston College's quarterback: "Even if he cannot make it in the pros he has a fine future ahead of him [The only place to have one, I've always said]. He has applied for a road scholarship and if it goes like everything else he does, he'll get it." Cecil Rhodes or Jack Kerouac, it's all educational, I guess.

And this from an interview with a local athlete, who is quoted as saying: "My freshman year, I wore glasses. I always wanted to look into contacts. At first I was told I had a stigmatism and I couldn't wear them." Even one stigmatism is alot.

The homophone problem here is particularly interesting to those who have studied our adoption of Latin phrases, as for example in adjourning a court *sine die* (a term the *Ninth New Collegiate* enters not in its section on foreign words and phrases, but in the main alphabet). Here we can see Latin become English right before our very eyes, as the *Campus* reporter wrote, "Lawlor's design is a graphic and creative work and also a bonified, enlightening advertisement for the 'Women in the Arts' Series." I suspect that the analogy must be with words like *verified*.

I'll end with this one: "Angelou . . . also encouraged students to 'have enough courage to love somebody . . . and then have the unmitigated gaul to accept love back.'" Is there a three-part kind?

CHAPTER 12

Professor Bolinger, Mr. Buckley, and King Canute

Most of what I'm describing as linguistic change and variation can, with social values added, also be called *usage*, a term that has been variously defined and much argued about over the past twenty years. The idea that usage or custom or what "they" (whoever "they" may be) are saying or writing is what sets the standard of language use has been vigorously attacked and vigorously defended. In chapter 2 I said a bit about the loudest and the longest sustained outcry thus far in this century: the contretemps following the publication of Merriam's 1961 unabridged dictionary, *Webster III*.

Language conservatives attacked the book for being permissive, for recording colloquial expressions and worse as though they were perfectly acceptable to every user and for every use. To the conservatives there seemed almost certainly to be a conspiracy among lexicographers and linguists: they seemed determined to agree that in language, "whatever is is right." Such an echo of Dr. Pangloss's "best of all possible worlds" folly gave no comfort to those who would resist *any* change and who were determined to preserve if they could the code of linguistic manners that had produced *their* language practices. They argued that the language didn't behave the way *Webster III*'s evidence pictured it, or that if for some reason language *did* behave that way, well, it *needn't*, and, by God, it *shouldn't*. And no one should accept a dictionary that pandered or gave even tacit approval to such breaches of what was clearly right and proper! Some conservatives wistfully and others angrily complained that nice semantic distinctions were being lost just because hordes of uncouth adults and untaught youths were being permitted to set the tone of the language and were letting in all sorts of barbarisms which no one of taste and maturity could countenance.

New guides to usage and new dictionaries representing a fairly wide range of social and political opinion on these issues have appeared in considerable numbers over the ensuing twenty years or so, and they're still coming, still arguing the matter. One of these new dictionaries, *American Heritage II* (1982), includes in its front matter two very brief essays which manage to put the usage issue more succinctly and more clearly than I've ever seen it handled before. The editors introduce these essays by remarking, "The opposing views set out in these essays will acquaint the reader with some of the issues that must be considered when a point of usage is in dispute" (30). This seems to me precisely the case.

In their essays, Dwight Bolinger, Emeritus Professor of Romance Languages and Literatures, Harvard University, and William F. Buckley, Jr., author, editor, pundit, and television personality, debate the following resolution:

Resolved: The prevailing usage of its speakers should be the chief determinant of acceptability in language. (30)

Both essays are brief and persuasively argued; my short summaries of their main arguments here cannot do full justice to the conviction and wit of their prose. Nonetheless, even short summaries can highlight the points of agreement and difference, can illustrate what an important issue usage is, and can thus make clearer to us the kinds of evidence and sorts of judgment that should help us form our attitudes toward these kinds of linguistic change and variation.

For the affirmative, Bolinger says, "Usage . . . is always the determinant of correctness" (30). He speaks of "the universe of conventions" (30) everyone follows, and points out that comparatively few of these conventions are in dispute. Then comes the question of what *prevailing* may mean—"the prevailing usage of its speakers." *Where* do particular usages prevail? In which of the many different constituencies to which users of the language can belong will we find them? He reminds us of the constituencies shaped in part by region, social class, age, sex, and the like, as well as those created by the particular occasion for speech or writing. The strength of "the past" and especially of "the literary past" in reaching normative judgments, Bolinger says, brings us to "where the sticky choices are usually made" (31). He talks too of some of the effects created by the shibboleths that constituencies will set up in order to keep interlopers out.

Normative Grammar is a hit-or-miss enterprise. Not that it needs to be—a more careful analysis and a heavier investment in teaching the language might make it an effective stabilizer. But there will be little enthusiasm for that as long as stigmatizing a few usages makes an effective test of social acceptability. [Here's Veblen's view of spelling yet again.]
In this small corner of the language a minority of the highbrow and the well-born may succeed in conferring authority on a small number of usages. Meanwhile a hundred times as many others are fluctuating undetected, with their success or failure guaranteed by majority usage in their constituencies. And common to all constituencies is the great semi-inert mass of usage where no conflict arises because everyone already obeys. (31–32)

Bolinger ends his argument for the affirmative thus:

Does this self-contained universe of usage ultimately decide what is acceptable? When Margaret Fuller proclaimed in 1846, "I accept the universe," Thomas Carlyle delivered his now-famous retort, "She'd better." (32)

For the negative, Buckley asserts that "precision in definition and inflection is still possible; and precision is still possible precisely because mere usage, however prolonged, does not baptize" (32). His religious figure, from which we are to infer the sinners on the one hand and the saved on the other, leads to his statement that we can know when dispensation is granted only by asking people like Buckley and others of his self-defined constituency (Bolinger's word, not Buckley's).

Buckley insists that "acceptability is by no means routinely achieved merely by democratic affirmation" (33). He argues that although the lexicographic purists "of this world cannot be permitted to freeze a language in its tracks, when changes are authorized they must be authorized by [those] of this world who [are capable of judging] . . . , because they are expertly trained and congenitally gifted. They know how to take careful measurements, and they use the language to do this" (33). One wonders if he thinks that lexicographers reach their conclusions by some different method; they too must use the language to do it. Most good lexicographers are "expertly trained," so one can only conclude that what lexicographers lack are the "congenital gifts." Pity. But, quite rightly,

Buckley reiterates, "the question is always, acceptance by whom?" (33). Bolinger's point is that not one but many constituencies, and combinations of many constituencies, accept various usages for various purposes and audiences.

Buckley finishes with a flourish for the negative:

> *Vulgar, Slang, Regional, Nonstandard, Informal:* most new meanings or uses need to work their way against that upstream drag; and resistance should be formal, i.e., embodied in a dictionary prepared to accept but also prepared to deny.
>
> Lexicographers are sufficiently conversant with their craft to make judgments, yea, even unto designating a word, or a usage, *illiterate.* The other way is mobocratic, undifferentiated. And what is the purpose of a *guide* to usage if not—as required—to exclude? The negative function of a dictionary is part of its function. It is not a sign of arrogance for the king to rule. That is what he is there for. (33)

And, one supposes, kings—especially philosopher-kings—are very likely to have been given the necessary congenital gifts.

Both writers make succinct, persuasive statements. And, of course, they are in considerable agreement, once we understand that they have very different ideas about the makeup of the constituencies of those who should form and judge the language. And, whereas Bolinger implies that if a cluster of major constituencies of users concludes that a usage he may find unpleasant or tasteless is nonetheless acceptable, he'll probably have to go along, however reluctantly (he'd better), Buckley confidently implies that if there is evidence of consensus in constituencies other than his own, but leading to a conclusion he doesn't like, he can ignore such evidence. (Kings are more equal than others.)

Perhaps this parable may help: King Canute and his English-Danish court were standing on the seashore, and his sycophantic followers were telling him what a great king he was. He ruled a kingdom whose lands stretched far on both sides of the North Sea, a kingdom that seemed to them unmatched in greatness. Indeed, they assured him, no one and nothing could withstand his power.

But Canute the Great was also wise. He chided his retinue for exaggerating and insisted that there was much in this world over which he could not rule. But they protested that this was quite untrue. Then Canute turned and strode to the very edge of the incoming tide, and raising both hand and voice to the sea, he commanded it to intrude no farther on the sands, lest the rising waters wet his feet. A short time later, the waters swirling about his knees, Canute turned silently and waded back up the sands to a dry place beyond the tide. Thus did this wise king demonstrate to his foolish followers that every man—the greatest of kings not least—must know the limits of his powers.

Buckley says, "It is not a sign of arrogance for the king to rule. That is what he is there for" (33). There is no quarrel with that, so long as the king knows what indeed he *can* rule. The Buckleys of this world have television cameras and microphones and printing presses at their service, and thus, like great kings, they have more power than most men over many man-made things, including much of manners. Thus they do have unusual power over some aspects of usage. They can often be tastemakers. They can sometimes set the standards for certain highly visible signs of what they deem good or true or beautiful. And congenital gifts will no doubt help them win the attention and the agreement of other, less-favored men. Sometimes, indeed, the courtiers will pay attention, and will say, "Yes, O King."

But, as Bolinger reminds us, it's best to accept universes we cannot change. Which is to say, as does King Canute, that there are larger rules and greater powers than those that kings may wield. Sometimes the accumulations of custom and convention, moving with the glacier's speed but with its force as well, have powers as irresistible as the tide's. For example, conservatives like Buckley may indeed cause members of their literate and congenitally gifted tongs to hate *hopefully* as an introductory adverbial sentence modifier; the conservative *American Heritage II* gives a fair picture of the analogy, but then urges that we avoid affronting traditionalists:

Usage: The use of *hopefully* to mean "it is to be hoped," as in *hopefully we'll get there before dark*, is grammatically justified by analogy to the similar uses of *happily* and *mercifully*. However, this usage is by now such a bugbear to traditionalists that it is best avoided on grounds of civility, if not logic.

Civility—even being nice to the king and supporting his whims—may seem perfectly reasonable to some or even to many. But in language change, analogy is a very strong force indeed, and when it sweeps in like a tide, most of the users of a language will forget that the king doesn't like it. Thus we find the situation we face with *hopefully*: if sizable numbers of otherwise civil people are unaware that there is anything in that locution that could grate on the feelings of the king, or if, despite his objections it still sounds all right to them, then even with the best will in the world, they will not follow the king. And if the king be not wise, he will be overwhelmed by the tide.

It is true, as we demonstrated in our discussion of the double negative (chap. 9), that sometimes the king and his henchmen can rule for wrong reasons or none, *and make it stick*. But these instances are rare. More frequently, if we would be kings, the best we can do is discipline ourselves the way good manners suggest, and then hope that if what we seek be* good, true, and beautiful, it may also be acceptable and workable. But if it be neither acceptable nor workable, for whatever reason, then we may find ourselves as kings sometimes have found themselves before, crying, "Forward!" and rushing into battle only to discover on looking back that no one is following. It's a wise king who knows which rules he may set.

The usage issue will never go away, and it will sometimes be willfully distorted. Recognizing, however ruefully, that a change we do not like has occurred in spite of our efforts to prevent it, we still have choice of action: we can gracefully concede the change; or we can reluctantly accept others' use of it, but quietly and firmly resolve to adhere to the old practice ourselves; or we can remain militantly and loudly opposed to the new and determined to reinstate the old. If the change is already complete or nearly so, this last option is quixotic, but it is probably no more evil than it will be effective. Besides, Don Quixote did have his admirers, even though he had only a few real followers. And as regards either of the other options: Sancho Panza's kind of common sense is by no means always reprehensible or self-serving, even when measured against the Don's idealism; sometimes, indeed, Sancho's way is in the best interests of clear discourse, civil justice, and peace.

When I returned to teaching, I wasn't surprised to find the usage

---

*I used subjunctive *be* two or three times in this paragraph and the one preceding. Most Americans would probably reserve it for legal documents, the pulpit, and (perhaps) parables, and use *is* instead on other occasions. What would you have used? And did you notice the *be* on p. 101?

issue bubbling and frothing away almost as fiercely as it had been in 1966 when I left. But I find both dictionaries and the people who make them are much more interested today than they were before in making certain that everyone who consults them on points of difficulty and divided usage has as much guidance as can be given: I find many more examples of balanced evaluation of the evidence and thoughtful, judicious suggestion as to what to do under a range of circumstance.

For example, *American Heritage II*'s usage note on *hopefully* is as precise a set of guidelines as one could find an unhappy conservative like Buckley giving (although I do not of course know his opinion on this usage). And I suspect that a liberal like Bolinger (whose opinion on this item I don't know either), while he would find little to cavil at in the assessment of the evidence *American Heritage II* provides, would probably still prefer (no matter what his personal practice with this usage might be) the *Ninth New Collegiate*'s advice to the user:

usage Only the irrationally large amount of critical fire drawn by sense 2 [it is hoped] of *hopefully* requires its particular recognition in a dictionary. Similar use of other adverbs (as *interestingly, presumably, fortunately*) as sentence modifiers is so commonplace as to excite no notice whatever. While it still arouses occasional objection, *hopefully* as a sentence modifier has been in use at least since 1932 and is well established as standard.

"Not *our* standard," cry the conservatives of this world. "It does not yet have *our* acceptance!"

"But it does have ours," choruses a sizable group of other speakers and writers, including some who share many of the conservatives' opinions on other points of usage.

Buckley says, "It doesn't matter if 99 percent of the American people say 'spokesperson.' Only if Kendall [a colleague at *National Review*]—and I—agree will it become 'acceptable'" (32). Buckley doesn't say whether they agree on it or not. I consulted our college dictionaries. *New World II* and *Random House Revised* do not have entries for *spokesperson*; presumably the word was too new at their dates of publication (1980 for the most recent printings I have of each, but their current editions are 1970 and 1975 respectively). But both *American Heritage II* (1982) and *Ninth New Collegiate* (1983) have entries for it, and neither gives it any sort of limiting label. *Spokesperson* has undoubtedly arrived in Standard English (as described by both conservative and liberal lexicographers), whether Buckley and friend have awarded it their imprimatur yet or not. For the record, to the complexity of the picture I ought to add the following: I myself never use the word except ironically (see p. 99 above), but on that issue at least, I do know where I stand with respect to the tide.

CHAPTER 13

A Miscellany of Change: Usage

Some usage problems are tough to decide; others are easy, especially once you've learned to judge the tides and the king's whims. And change and variation can affect any part of a living language: vocabulary, inflections and other aspects of morphology (the shapes and forms of words), pronunciations, spellings, and syntax (word order, empty "function words," and the way we string words together). Here are a few quite random examples of kinds of change and variation and our attitudes toward them; these too became apparent to me on my return.

One of the most powerful generalizations we can make about the English language is that over the centuries the language has steadily been losing its inflections—those endings that tell us about a word's case, number, gender, or some other grammatical feature. Today's English has fewer cases, fewer declensions, and fewer distinctive numbers than did Old English, and it has no inflections at all for gender except in the third-person singular pronouns; long ago Old English had gender in inflections on nouns, pronouns, adjectives, and demonstratives. Because this trend of loss of inflections has long been well established, one of the first things I sought to check on when I returned was the state of English inflections: what else had disappeared? Had the twenty years brought much in the way of further loss?

That generalization—that English continues to lose its inflections—is still accurate. But the process has always been slow, and twenty years is a very short time for most inflectional changes to complete themselves, particularly in light of another generalization about the disappearance of inflections: the fewer the inflections left and the higher their frequency of use, the less likely they are to disappear.

Whom, the objective (accusative) case form of the pronoun and function word *who*, is an interesting illustration of this sort of change, and its use seems to have dwindled perceptibly during the past twenty years. The *who/whom* quandary also demonstrates very nicely some of the roles played by the generations in matters of usage of this kind. Back in the 1960s the schools were still trying to teach the young to use *whom* wherever an objective case was called for, regardless of situation or audience or syntax. The workbooks usually insisted on *Whom were you with?* and so did those school-teachers—a dwindling number even then—who had fully mas-tered the usage themselves. They insisted on it not only in the pupils' writing but in their recitations as well, although some of these teachers recognized that what they frequently called "slovenliness" (*who* being heard where the structure required the objective case *whom*) was often "tolerated" in very casual or infor-mal speech. Observant, objective teachers found the practice in their own informal usage as well. In general, however, the majority of speakers of everyday English and some who tried to speak Standard English had already much reduced their use of *whom* in some direct object functions. Now, still more of *whom* seems to me to have worn away.

My impression today is that in speech at all levels of formality and in all but the most formal kinds of writing, *whom* has practi-cally disappeared except when it is *clearly* in objective "territory," as for example when it is tucked in directly behind a preposition: *To whom did you give it?* None of my students today would say *With who did you go?* But they'll use *who* every time if the preposition wanders away: *Who did you go with?* As a relative pronoun, as in *He's the one who, after some hesitation, we asked to drive, who/ whom* has a much more variable distribution in current practice; in most speech and in some writing, many people today will use the unchanging *that* form, or no relative at all, perhaps, just to avoid a difficult choice. And in situations where they *do* employ one, we'll often find *whom* and *whomever* in places where we'd expect *who* or *whoever* (*Ask whomever won the prize*); these are the usages of those who've been taught there's a problem, but who have not retained— if they have ever really learned—the older "correct" pattern. These are the "mistakes" of the self-conscious, and they tell us a good deal about the state of the usage item itself. If people are particular-ly concerned about making the right choice, they'll frequently choose consciously, and they'll frequently overcorrect; if they're not much concerned, they'll probably use *who* unconsciously in a situation like this—and be accidentally "right." It seems to me that the smaller number of overcorrections among my students these days shows that they're much less worried about this usage than were their parents twenty-odd years ago.

Much the same force is at work in *Who did she marry?* and in that old chestnut, *It's me* (or *him*, or *her*, or *them*). Syntax is now providing much of the grammatical information formerly supplied by inflections now weakened or lost. Position in the sentence can frequently override the signals sent by inflections, and that overriding seems to be getting stronger. When Old English nouns had distinctive nominative and objective case inflections, we could put the words anywhere in the sentence and still tell subjects from objects. Nouns now have only two cases—an uninflected all-purpose one and a possessive (or genitive) one using some form of the -*s* inflection. Therefore, it's only in pronouns that we have the ability to distinguish between nominative and objective, and with a few pronouns, such as *you* and *it*, we can't choose a case-distinctive nominative or accusative form at all. But for grammatical meaning, for the all-important purpose of distinguishing subjects from objects, position in the sentence has become more important than ever. The small boy's tearful *Him hit me!* leaves no doubt that, objective case or not, *him* is the subject. So it's no wonder that the speakers of the vulgate often say things like *I thought they were calling her and I* and *Fred and me was at the store.* If there's a conflict between syntax and case, word order will usually override inflections. For these reasons we shouldn't be surprised to find *who* appearing in nearly all beginning-of-the-sentence spots in the vulgate. But more important, today we'll usually hear it there in much Standard English too.

Then, since both *who* and *whom* are also the question-asking function words that so frequently lead off questions, and since they also serve as the relative pronouns at the beginnings of relative clauses, *who* is increasingly getting the call over *whom* in nearly all such other front locations except the most formal, regardless of whether the word would parse out as subject or object. *Who did she marry? The girl who the dogs chased got away.*

These changes are to some extent practiced by most of us; they are absolutely true of the younger generations, as I say. Some of us in the older generations can still accurately manage the classic distribution of *whom* at least some of the time, but often, especially in speech, we still overcorrect: *Whom shall I say is calling?* As all uncertain golfers know, in correcting your slice, you often develop a terrible hook to replace it. Members of my generation may also remember radio's young Henry Aldrich's broken-voiced adolescent cry of injured innocence: "Who, I?"

The generalization about the disappearance of inflections is still accurate and powerful: *whom* continues to wear away. Also still accurate is the generalization that the fewer but more frequently used the remaining distinctive forms, the more likely we are to hang onto them; we're quite likely to keep using *whom* immediately after prepositions, just as we continue to use certain frozen bits of the subjunctive, such as *If I were you,* . . . . The generalizations are important, but so are close inspections of the details.

So, it won't surprise you to learn that another usage item I examined as soon as I got back was the subjunctive. When I left teaching in 1966, the subjunctive was already much reduced in use, and I was interested to see that the trend has continued and that a bit more of it is gone today. Present and past subjunctive show somewhat different patterns of erosion. *If he be ready to join, why is he not present?* would almost never occur today. In the present tense, the indicative *If he is ready to join,* . . . would probably be the choice, with the subjunctive past (and present?) *If he were ready* . . . also possible. But in the past tense, almost the only form we'll find today is the past indicative: *If he was ready to join,* . . . .

With verbs other than *be*, there's only one subjunctive form left, the third-singular present tense, and we hear it rarely: *If he have time, he will* . . . or *If he think clearly, he must* . . . just don't get said much any more, except perhaps from the pulpit. Instead, we regularly get the indicatives *has* and *thinks* or perhaps the infinitive forms of these verbs following an auxiliary like *should,* as in *If he should have time,* . . . and *If he should think,* . . . .

But diminished though it may be, like *whom*, the subjunctive is by no means dead. In the formal request *I asked that he telephone his mother*, in the parliamentary motion *I move that he be declared the winner*, and in the stereotyped *If I were you*, we find the subjunctive fairly consistently in use in Standard English. Nor does there seem to be much likelihood that these instances will atrophy soon and fall off. With so little of the subjunctive left, those who wish to police it will find it much easier to enforce, perhaps, than when there was a great deal of divided usage in constructions that had once called for it. We're getting down now to some very simple matters. The frequency of use of indicatives or auxiliaries in places where, a generation ago, Standard English speakers and particularly writers of Standard English would have used a subjunctive is now overwhelmingly higher than the occurrence of subjunctives. So the bets are that with the exceptions noted, we'll find the use of the subjunctive with verbs other than *be* will continue to dwindle. But we'll also find that the stereotypical uses of the subjunctive will very likely hang on for a long time to come, if not indefinitely.

Other shapes besides these changed while I was gone. Many morphological changes seem to have proceeded further along paths they were already on when I had last examined them. *Dove* as the past tense of *dive* (instead of *dived*) was already a solid favorite in New England twenty years ago, but in my classes I used to find divided usage to be fairly common among Northern dialect speakers from the far western side of Connecticut. Today, however, almost every one of my students uses *dove*, and only one or two have *dived* even as a divided usage. Many claim that they've never heard *dived* at all. The *Ninth New Collegiate*'s usage note seems to me not a bit too hasty in giving status:

> *Dive*, which was orig. a weak verb, developed a past tense *dove*, prob. by analogy with verbs like *drive, drove*. . . . Linguistic geographers indicate that its use in the U.S. is expanding. Although *dived* is somewhat more common in writing in the U.S. and is usual in British English, *dove* must be considered an acceptable variant.

And, I would add, in New England, *dove* is almost the only game in town for natives.

Snuck as a past tense and past participle of *sneak* was considered a vulgate word by most of my colleagues and many of my students twenty years ago, although it regularly occurred then in student speech. *Sneaked* was the preferred form in those days, especially in writing, at least for those who didn't seek a circumlocution in order to avoid having to make any choice at all. Today, most of my students use *snuck* in both speech and writing, and several of them are skeptical of my assurance that I regularly use *sneaked* and have never said *snuck* "without putting quotes around it." But I heard CBS anchorman Dan Rather use it on the tube on two occasions early in the summer of 1985. It's clear today that *snuck* has achieved status in the eyes of all but the most rigorously conservative. *Ninth New Collegiate* cites both forms, listing *sneaked* first but giving no usage advice or other label. Back in 1963, Merriam's *Seventh New Collegiate* didn't even list *snuck* as a possible variant, but its parent *Webster III* included the form and called it *"chiefly dial."* The form, dialectal or generally vulgate, has clearly been around for some time. Mencken had it in his list of vulgate verb forms in the fourth edition of *The American Language* in 1945 (435). The point I find most interesting is that liberal lexicographers have concluded that in less than twenty years the form has come from a clearly recognized vulgate status to something like full acceptability. Yet *American Heritage II* is unconvinced: its entry for *snuck* (1982) is labeled *"Nonstandard."** That's a rose-colored glasses view, I think; both *New World II* and *Random House Revised* are older books than *American Heritage II*, but both agree with *Ninth New Collegiate* that the *snuck* form is now standard. The word has made it with all but the very conservative.

Another morphological development is the very rapid change in the way the word *kudos* behaves. In 1958 *ACD* handled the word very economically; there were no problems: "kū' dos), *n.* glory; renown. [t. Gk.: m. k*y*dos]." Only one pronunciation was offered, the first syllable rhyming with *two*, the second (unstressed) with the first vowel of *father*, and there was no note on usage. By 1969, after commenting that the word was "Originally British university slang, from Greek *kudos*, glory, fame," *American Heritage* noted: "*Kudos* is construed as singular in the choice of a verb: *Kudos is due him.* The singular term *kudo*, which is not acceptable in standard usage, is the invention of those who misconstrue *kudos* as exclusively plural." The eggheaded origin of the word in English—university slang—suggests that most of the early users of the slang, at least,

---

*William and Mary Morris, in *Dictionary of Contemporary Usage*, 2d ed., call it "a dialect variant," "admissible only in informal contexts, usually as a bit of jocosity" (554).

would have been aware that the Greek word was singular, despite its ending in -*s* and consequently looking like a regular English plural. The catch of course for those who didn't know Greek was that in Greek it didn't *sound* like an English plural. A final syllable rhyming with *dose* or *moss* is clearly singular in English, but the increasingly frequent pronunciation of *kudos* rhyming with *doze* is just as clearly a regular English plural, from which we may then infer a regular singular, *kudo*, whether everyone wants to accept it or not. We call the process *back-formation*.

As the *Ninth* points out in its excellent usage note on *kudo* as a back-formation, "It may have begun as a misunderstanding, but then so did *cherry* and *pea*." And when we consult the *Ninth* about *cherry*, we learn that it derives from Old North French *cherise*, a singular that was taken as a plural in Middle English and so led via back-formation to the singular, Middle English *chery*; *pea*, the *Ninth* tells us, came from Middle English *pease*, a singular that was taken as plural and so led to a back-formation, *pea*, as singular. That *cherries* and *peas* are more readily available than *kudos* undoubtedly makes a difference in the ease with which the new form slips into the standard language, but the implications of the process are pretty clear in all three instances.

The regular pattern for forming plural nouns in English is very powerful. English has regularly manufactured back-formations, and although sometimes some of them have had a hard time winning approval, even the low-frequency or learned words of this sort, such as *resurrect*, *donate*, *execute*, and *enthuse*, eventually, like *pea* and *cherry*, became satisfactory to nearly everyone. *Enthuse* has perhaps encountered more resistance than the others. *American Heritage II* still labels it *informal*, which is a considerable relaxation of the implications of its predecessor's 1969 usage note describing the usage panel's disapproval:

> *Enthuse* is not well established in writing on a serious level. The following typical examples are termed unacceptable by substantial majorities of the Usage Panel. *The majority leader enthused over his party's gains* is disapproved by 76 per cent. *He was considerably less enthused by signs of factionalism* is disapproved by 72 per cent. Alternative phrasing might be *became* or *waxed enthusiastic* or *was less enthusiastic over*.

There may still be a few of the entrenched elderly who have no enthusiasm for *enthuse*, but their days like their powers are failing and will soon end.

I've found many trifling but amusing illustrations of semantic change over the past twenty years, some of them very clearly a combination of changes in the meaning of the referent of the word and differences in what older and younger generations' experiences with the referent have been. The following example also includes an interesting modification of pronunciation.

Arctic, pronounced "artick," has long been with us as an alternative pronunciation, but twenty years ago that pronunciation was considered acceptable (if at all) only for the galoshes, not for the geographical area to our north or for the adjective applied to it. Interestingly enough, today "articks" are still galoshes for those of us who remember that name for the winter footgear which few seem to wear any more, but I found on my return that many of my students not only don't pronounce the medial *k*-sound but haven't any idea what *arctics*, however you pronounce them, are! The *Ninth New Collegiate* still gives for the cold region, adjective and noun, a first pronunciation with the medial *k*-sound and a second without it, exactly the reverse of the order it reports for the pronunciations of the overshoes. Here then is a fairly trivial generational difference, aided by a loss of currency in one meaning of the word. The generations are no longer in accord, and a reasonable guess would be that in a generation or two, the medial *k*-sound in both geographic and "overshoes" meanings will be archaic if not obsolete.

Another example, this time more complex, from among dozens we might examine, further illustrates the powerful role our varying constituencies play. Bolinger suggested that among them we might recognize region, social class, age, sex, voluntary association, setting, occasion, and medium (*American Heritage II*, 30); I'd stress especially the generations (age) and the various aspects of the situation (setting, occasion, medium), including audience. The last twenty years of the history of *less* and *fewer*, with the grating on elderly and conservative ears of "Less calories!" and the like, display a familiar pattern. In 1960 Margaret Bryant summarized her survey of usage studies on *less* with count nouns thus: "*Less occurs with countable items in magazines and formal texts. In one study*, less *was so employed in 20% of the examples; in another, in 33% of them. Evidence shows that usage is divided"* (129). Around 1960 the college dictionaries reflected that divided usage, although all were fairly calm. *Sixth New Collegiate* and *New World* made no mention of any problem, giving straightforward definitions of *few* and *less*. In its entry for *less*, the Funk and Wagnalls *College Standard* (1956) commented in its definition for its sense three: "Fewer: used with collective nouns. *Less* refers to quantity, measure, or degree; *fewer* refers to number." There was no suggestion that these entries posed any particular problem, nor was there any indication that the editors saw this usage item's developing ere long into a full-fledged dilly.

Perhaps the most thorough treatment of the *less/fewer* issue in the college dictionaries of the early 1960s is *ACD*'s (1958); in a synonymy following the entry for *fewer*, we find the following:

FEWER, LESS are sometimes confused because both imply a comparison with something larger (in number or in amount). FEWER applies only to number: *fewer street cars are running now than ten years ago.* LESS is used in various ways. It is commonly applied to material in bulk, in reference to amount: *less gasoline in the tank than we thought.* It is also used frequently with abstractions, esp. where the idea of amount is figuratively present: *less courage, less wealth.* LESS applies where such attributes as value, degree, etc. (but not size or number) are concerned: *a nickel is less than a dime* (in value); *a corporal is less than a sergeant* (in rank).

In one respect the distinction seemed clear: use *fewer* with number, and *less* for everything else. That oversimplification may in part explain the confusion *ACD* referred to: if *less* were to be used in a great number of situations, then there would be a temptation to use it in all, perhaps. One other problem was and is the antonym, *more*. Alas, it works acceptably with *both* mass and count nouns: *more money, more dollars; more chickens and eggs, more poultry and fish.* So why shouldn't *less* work the same way? In 1961 and 1963, *Webster III* and *Seventh New Collegiate* made no particular point about usage; they merely defined *less* and *fewer*; there was neither synonymy nor usage note to suggest that a hard choice might await the user.

By 1969 *American Heritage* had wheeled out its usage panel; this distinction, in *American Heritage*'s view, was clearly one that deserved careful explanation and firm advice to the reader. Its usage note detailed the distinction between *fewer* for numbers and *less* for quantity, with examples and percentages (67 percent to 77 percent) of the usage panel members who found typical uses of *less* with numbers unacceptable, not just less preferable. Further, one example at the end of the usage note illustrates the crumbling foundations on which this distinction in some uses rests: "*less than 50 feet.*" Consider the "collective sense" of these: *The house had less than fifty feet of frontage. The insect had fewer than fifty feet on each side.*

Today, *Random House Revised* and *New World II* provide neither advice nor usage label. But *American Heritage II* has become firmer than before: clearly, no more patient Mr. Nice Guy; the usage note is terse and specific, decreeing *fewer* for numbers and *less* for mass, although noting that this distinction is apparently maintained fully only in writing. Twenty years ago such was not the case, at least as the dictionaries saw it; there was no division in usage between speech and writing; it was just a question then of knowing apples from orange juice: *fewer numbers, less mass.*

But the last word, at least from the college dictionaries, probably ought to be the *Ninth New Collegiate*'s; at least it's the most recent view. Here again we get a combination of history and candor in the usage note following the entry for *less*:

The traditional view is that *less* applies to matters of degree, value, or amount and modifies collective nouns, mass nouns, or nouns denoting an abstract whole while *fewer* applies to matters of number and modifies plural nouns. *Less* has been used to modify plural nouns since the days of King Alfred and the usage, though roundly decried, appears to be increasing.

The *Ninth* and I agree with *American Heritage II* that failure to maintain the distinction has been "roundly decried"; to many in the older generation *less calories* grates horribly; but it seems equally clear, despite *Heritage II*'s panel, that the use of *less* to modify plural nouns (*less calories, less vitamins*) is increasing, heading perhaps back toward its status in Alfred's time, where it apparently could be so used without cavil.

Many semantic changes have also caught my attention since my return. *Notoriety* has caught both my eye and ear during the last year or two. It seems to have begun to lose much of its pejorative loading, at least on the sports pages, in the chatter on radio and television, and in the conversation of my students and a good many other adults. In 1958 *ACD* said that the most common meaning of *notoriety* was "state or character of being notorious or widely known," and then defined *notorious* first as "widely but unfavorably known," and second as simply "publicly or generally known." *ACD*, remember, made a great point of its putting the most common current meanings first, followed by older, and then archaic and obsolete meanings, in that order. It put the pejorative sense of *notorious* first.

Seventh New Collegiate's 1963 definition of *notoriety* also depended upon its definition of *notorious*, the adjective, which it defined as "generally known and talked of; *esp*: widely and unfavorably known." In a cross-reference to a synonymy at *famous*, the *Seventh* reported, "NOTORIOUS frequently adds to FAMOUS an implication of questionableness or evil." So, both *ACD* and the *Seventh* considered the word at the very least to be "frequently" pejorative. But it's pretty clear too that prior to *Webster III* (1961), some dictionaries considered the "generally known and talked of" meaning, when it occurred without any pejorative coloration, to be used chiefly in Britain. Today, however, my eye and ear tell me that even though the most recent of all the college dictionaries, *Ninth New Collegiate*, reprints essentially the 1963 entry for *notoriety*, there is a growing current use of the word, in informal speech and in journalism, with that nonpejorative meaning. "Generally known and talked of," minus any sense of "unfavorably known," seems to me to be increasingly popular. It appears that only the abstract noun, *notoriety*, and not the adjective, *notorious*, is undergoing this semantic change. Far more athletes are winning *notoriety* in the sports pages these days than can be truly *notorious*, it seems to me, although the college dictionaries so far seem not to have found enough evidence yet to support my conclusions in their entries. But many sports writers today think notoriety is a good thing.

Enormity, another of those abstract nouns with a pejorative flavor, appears to have undergone a good deal of elevation over the past twenty years or so, too. For many speakers today, it means simply "the quality of being enormous, or very big indeed," with none of the suggestion of monstrosity or heinousness it carried twenty and more years ago. That this semantic change is still in progress, and that some people, at least, are by no means willing to admit that it *is* taking place and certainly don't *want* it to take place, can be illustrated again from the college dictionaries.

In 1958 ACD gave the most common meaning of *enormity* as "outrageous or heinous character; atrociousness: the *enormity of his offenses,*" and as a second, presumably less common meaning, "something outrageous or heinous, as an offense." Both senses were clearly pejorative as ACD saw them. By 1963 *Seventh New Collegiate* defined the oldest sense of *enormity* as "the quality or state of being immoderate, monstrous, or outrageous; *esp*: a great wickedness." Its second meaning was also pejorative: "a grave offense." But its third and latest meaning was simply "HUGENESS, IMMENSITY," both synonyms lacking the clearly pejorative qualities of the two older senses.

Today's *American Heritage II* (1982) does not agree that *Seventh New Collegiate*'s third meaning exists. In its entry for *enormity* we find only two meanings: "1. The quality of passing all moral bounds; excessive wickedness or outrageousness. 2. A monstrous offense or evil; outrage." Here is no sign of the simple, uncharged idea of great size, no sign of the amelioration of the word in any sense.

Yet just a few years ago I heard the president of a large university comment publicly on the occasion of a long-time administrator's stepping down from his post, and in what I took to be generous— perhaps even fulsome—praise, he spoke of "the enormity" of what the departing man had done during his years as an administrator. The pejorative sense of the word is certainly not gone, but clearly it is not the only or necessarily even the most popular meaning any more.

Ninth New Collegiate has redefined its third (and most recent) meaning of *enormity*: "the quality or state of being huge: IMMENSITY." The usage note that follows is particularly germane to the question of change about which I've been puzzling:

Enormity, some people insist, is improperly used to denote large size and is properly used only to denote wickedness, outrage, or crime. They recommend *enormousness* for large size. *Enormousness*, however, is simply not a popular word. . . . *Enormity*'s third sense has continued in use from the end of the eighteenth century; it has been stigmatized as incorrect, for unknown reasons, since the end of the nineteenth. *Enormity* is used with more subtleness than is usu. indicated. In sense 1 it need not carry overtones of moral transgression, although it most often does. It regularly denotes a considerable departure from the expected or normal. . . . While it is used neutrally to denote great size, more often it is used of something so large as to be overwhelming the ⟨*enormity* of population pressures in India—M. T. Kaufman⟩ ⟨the *enormity* of the task of teachers in slum schools—J. B. Conant⟩ and may even be used to suggest both great size and deviation from morality.

But to me the point that appears to need making most of all is this: like *notoriety* in its relationship to *notorious*, so is *enormity* in its relationship to *enormous*: English has long had the ability to make abstract nouns of adjectives; this functional shift meets a need or it would not occur. But functional shifts frequently lead to semantic shifts as well, and to the divergence of meanings of the parent word and its offspring.

Then, too, we appear to overuse abstract nouns, as the Kaufman and Conant quotations in the *Ninth*'s usage note suggest. How much better and stronger the prose would be if the population pressures in India *are* or *grow enormous* or are just *India's enormous population pressures*, and how much better it would sound if the same could be said of the task of teachers in slum schools. Because we overuse *enormity*, we put it at semantic risk. And because *enormous* no longer carries the pejorative senses it once had (when it meant "ABNORMAL, INORDINATE," or "exceedingly wicked," as the *Ninth* observes), *enormity* tends to carry a related meaning and to lose some of its pejorative qualities too. Predictably, if university presidents—or some of them, anyway—no longer hear those pejorative overtones in the noun, and if we continue our infatuation with abstract nouns and prepositional phrase modifiers instead of seeking sharp, spare adjectives to modify our nouns, then it is highly unlikely that the noun *enormity* will carry any other meaning for most readers and listeners than that suggested by the most common meaning of *enormous*: huge, immense. Any intended pejorative overtones will fall on ears increasingly deaf to them.

One constant complaint of purists, conservatives, the entrenched elderly, and their sympathizers when I left teaching was that *disinterested* was constantly being misused to mean "indifferent," when everyone knew it really meant "impartial." The *disinterested/uninterested* usage problem was a kind of rallying point for all who loved tradition, virtue, and truth. It still is. But the evidence and the interpretation of it are such as to make the issue by no means so simple as most people assume it to be.

Both *disinterested* and *uninterested* are seventeenth-century additions to the vocabulary; then, *disinterested,* which seems to have come first, meant "indifferent," and *uninterested* meant "impartial, unbiased." In the eighteenth century, *disinterested* seems to have taken over the "impartial" sense and *uninterested* the "indifferent" meaning.

The 1960 *New World* gave two meanings for *disinterested,* the "impartial" sense first (as being the more common use) and the "uninterested, indifferent" sense second and labeled "[Colloq.]." In *New World II* the senses of the word are the same and are reported in the same order, but instead of the *colloquial* label on the "indifferent" sense, the editors gave us this information: *disinterested* "in this usage [is] a revival of an obsolete meaning."

The Random House dictionaries provide somewhat different advice. In the firm's *ACD,* the more common sense of *disinterested* was also "unbiased," but the "indifferent" second sense had a usage label: "U.S. Colloq." *Random House Revised* has the same two senses, but labels the second, "indifferent" sense "*Nonstandard,*" suggesting that its editors see stronger objection to the word than did their *ACD* predecessors, not just for written uses, but for all standard uses.

American Heritage had the same order of definitions for *disinterested,* labeled the second, "indifferent" sense "*Non-standard,*" and in a short usage note observed: "According to 93 per cent of the Usage Panel, *disinterested* is not acceptable in the sense of *uninterested* [*indifferent, not interested*], though it is often thus employed." But it was only so employed, *Heritage* thought, as a *nonstandard* locution. *American Heritage II* reads the situation as worsening from the conservatives' viewpoint: it has dropped the *nonstandard* label from sense 2, and in place of the usage panel's 93 percent, it now reports: "A majority of the Usage Panel insists that *disinterested* should not be used for *uninterested,* despite an increasing tendency to use the two words interchangeably." The distinction between the terms appears somehow to be slipping away, in spite of the panelists' and other conservatives' efforts.

Ninth New Collegiate describes the meanings similarly, but assesses the situation differently. Its long usage note on *disinterested* says in part:

> The original sense of *uninterested* [meaning "unbiased"] is still out of use, but the original sense of *disinterested* ["indifferent"] revived in the early 20th century. The revival has since been under frequent attack as an illiteracy and a blurring or loss of a useful distinction. Actual usage shows otherwise. Sense 2 of *disinterested* ["free from selfish motive or interest"] is still its most frequent sense, esp. in edited prose; it shows no sign of vanishing.

So this distinction is by no means doomed, as some fear. Incidentally, the *Ninth's* usage note shows that the Merriam editors have learned their lesson well: their response to that charge of "permissiveness" leveled at *Webster III* and the *Seventh* and *Eighth* collegiates is here in the *Ninth*, where they maintain their liberal assessment of usage, but in their notes provide details of history and nuance of use which I think are unmatched anywhere else, given the restrictions of space in this type of book.

I added this last usage item after I'd gotten my copyedited manuscript back from the publisher. My editor had changed to *that* some eighty uses of *which* which I'd used (as here) to introduce restrictive clauses. And in several other instances she had proposed that I drop the relative altogether. Her reason was that most of today's edited prose continues to preserve the distinction which Strunk and White (among others) describe as follows:

> *That. Which. That* is the defining or restrictive pronoun, *which* the nondefining, or nonrestrictive. . . .
>> The lawn mower that is broken is in the garage. (Tells which one)
>> The lawn mower, which is broken, is in the garage. (adds a fact about the only mower in question)
> The use of *which* for *that* is common in written and spoken language. . . .
> But it would be a convenience to all if these two pronouns were used with precision. The careful writer, watchful for small conveniences, goes *which*-hunting, removes the defining *whiches*, and by so doing improves his work. (59)

It's long been thought a good idea to preserve neat distinctions; we always hope that a natural language like English can take on some of the precision of an artificial language like mathematics. But even in 1926, H. W. Fowler recognized the difficulty; his nearly twelve columns on relative *that* begin:

> 1. Relation between *that* & *which*. What grammarians say should be has perhaps less influence on what shall be than even the more modest of them realize; usage evolves itself little disturbed by their likes & dislikes. And yet the temptation to show how better use might have been made of the material to hand is sometimes irresistible. The English relatives, more particularly as used by English rather than American writers, offer such a temptation. (635)

In 1985 the Morrises reported divided opinions between what their usage panel members think ought be done and what they actually do: about half the panel do not maintain the distinction between *that* and *which* in speech, although 68 percent say that they do in their writing; yet 62 percent of them believe the distinction worth preserving (578). Among their comments is Barbara Tuchman's telling wistful observation: "They would be worth preserving if only one could make the distinction more comprehensible. I have never been able to apply the rule because . . . I can't see any difference in the restrictive nature of the two clauses—so I always end up going by sound. I wish a good clear rule could be evolved" (579). Alas, only edited prose, edited by cultivated editors for cultivated readers, seems able uniformly to preserve it. Even if we want to do it, we can only edit it, not write it.

I find it interesting that the relatively liberal Merriam *Ninth New Collegiate*, although it gives many examples, offers no usage note on the choice, but that the relatively conservative *American Heritage II* provides long usage notes at the entries for both *that* and *which* to guide the reader toward the distinction.

So what did I do when my editor took so many exceptions to my uses of relatives? Before sending in the manuscript the first time, I myself had excised all the *whiches* that had grated on me when I reread them, but I'd left many more, apparently unnoticed by even my editorial ear and eye. Nonetheless, as many as a third of the readers of my edited prose may be those who find *which* in place of *that* (or no relative at all) unpleasant or worse. With editorial help, I can conform to their expectations; conformity to this rule, whether it's imaginary or not, gives me almost no pain, but may save some others from marred pleasures if not from real pain. That makes an easy choice most of the time.

But what I see is a further change in manners. Twenty years ago, gentlemen were married—a fairly formal occasion—in a pretty restricted choice of costumes, ranging from morning coat if the hour were right to restrained business suit if the occasion were modest. As everyone knows, today neither men's wedding clothes nor their other formal attire shows the same restraint in color, form, or decoration. Traditional clothes are still worn in some venues, and when that happens, the older generation often comes away musing, "How nice." But there's less of it all the time.

And so it is with the distinction between *that* and *which* as relatives. Fewer of us control the distinction under any circumstances today, and even those of us who can sometimes do so editorially, if not in the heat of composition, don't feel the need to do so very often. In submitting this manuscript to my editor, I found this time that I can no longer even *edit* out restrictive *which* unerringly. Therefore, it's another usage item which/that/(or *no* relative) I'm going to be studying carefully in future.

But let's take a final look at some of the implications of usage. Look again at *less* and *fewer*, for instance. It's clear that all this "round decrying" of current usage has come close to making a shibboleth of the distinction between *less* and *fewer*, if only for the entrenched elderly and those of other generations who may wish to follow them. But the angry older voices are becoming less powerful every year. The defenders of the distinction are more than embattled, it seems to me. They've fallen back to what may be their last line of defense, and they're dug in there on the written—especially the formal written—language's insistence on the full distinction. In this instance, however, I fear that the spoken language and the written language that imitates it in advertising and journalism and the arts have outflanked the defenders' final position. The shibboleth will perhaps remain effective for another generation or so; I have to die off, for one, although my missionary zeal now is pretty much limited to insisting that my students know that there are people out there still who, like me, would prefer that the distinction be kept. But I have to admit that we control fewer and fewer publishers and less and less of the press these days; our numbers are dwindling, and our effectiveness with them.

That, it turns out, is the most damnable thing about the generational conflict over usage. Just when we get the wisdom and dynastic desire to enforce our standards, our powers begin to wane, our voices weaken, and we die. It's not so much that most of us resent youth's being wasted on the young; I really don't want to trade places with them. But to some of us it seems a shame (and to others an outrage) that now that we know the truth at last, we no longer have the strength to enforce it on those whom we're sure it could benefit most. Yet when the proposition is stated that baldly, perhaps it doesn't seem quite so important that we prevail. Fortunately, natural language will see to it sometimes that we do, and then again sometimes that we do not. When we do, the double negative comes to mind: our enforcement is strong, and the manners sometimes stick, even if only to those who want them. For the rest, what works, works, and as always with speakers of the vulgate, there are more of them than there are of us, even if on occasion we can be "more equal than others" on a few issues.

An interesting sidelight is that with the aging of our American society, it may be true that there are coming to be more of us in the older generations than in the younger. That should be an increasingly interesting factor to weigh as we continue to examine usage. Certainly, we must never underestimate the strength or the persistence of the generational clashes over it.

This chapter has dealt with details, details of sounds, shapes, forms, meanings. Some of the changes we found are simply further variation in directions long established; others are changes apparently quite recent and relatively sudden. The point to be stressed is that we were examining kinds of change that took place in so short a time as twenty years.

What can we generalize from these few examples? Probably not a great deal more than the tentative suggestions we've made during the discussion of the details. In looking at *dove* and *snuck* we've seen the strong verb patterns for forming the preterit and past participle of the verb do something odd and unpredictable. The generalization we normally rely on here is that the weak verb pattern, the one with the dental suffix endings for preterit and past participle, is the productive one; we always build new verbs on that pattern, as these recent new verbs illustrate: *sardine (They sardined ten people into the little car)* ends its preterit and past principle with a -d sound; *shunpike* (*We had shunpiked rather than drive the interstates*) ends with a -t sound, and *redshirt* (*The coach redshirted him during his freshman year*) ends in an extra syllable with an -id sound. Over the long history of the language, the general trend has been for many strong verbs to be replaced by or turn into weak ones. Yet here we are reminded of the necessity for looking at details and not assuming that generalizations are laws.

In a few bits of detail about semantic change, we've noted how quickly—twenty years may be a lot for a Van Winkle, but it's a trifle in the long history of the English vocabulary—words can change their meanings and their status. One point particularly stands out: of all the aspects of language, vocabulary is the one that can change most rapidly. All aspects of a living language are constantly changing, mostly at very slow rates; but the lexicon can change quickly. Hence our need to look and listen closely. Hence also our need for frequent new editions of our college dictionaries.

Finally, we've seen the importance of our following both lines in studying the language: the details and the generalizations. After twenty years away, I've found ample evidence of the need to check out all the details, to evaluate each on its own merits, and then to test and perhaps modify those big generalizations about how the language works. It's my guess that if a Van Winkle stopped pretending to be disinterested and dove straight into this study, he'd end by discovering that he'd snuck right up on the truth, and he'd find that the enormity of his efforts had earned him those kudos that only they win who have achieved true notoriety.

CHAPTER 14

Bilingualism, Bidialectalism, and the Polyglot Boarding House

Not long ago I received a form letter signed by S. I. Hayakawa, the author, semanticist, former university president, and ex-senator from California, inviting me to join a group seeking to amend the U.S. Constitution to make English "the official language of the United States," and to specify that "neither the United States nor any state shall require . . . the use in the United States of any language other than English." I didn't join because I'm not much for amending the Constitution, but I did keep in touch with the group's efforts, which, as the months went by, began to get increasing coverage in the press.

Then George Will devoted his *Newsweek* column (8 July 1985, 78) to consideration of the proposed amendment, which he said would "prohibit governments from mandating multilingual publications and from establishing bilingual education as a general entitlement. It would end the pernicious practice of providing bilingual ballots." He concluded that the importance of the language issue probably does justify the means proposed—amending the Constitution.

But, you may ask, what on earth is this all about? Is the existence of other languages in this country something new? Has countenancing their presence here suddenly become unpatriotic? Haven't most of us been proud of our foreign heritages? Are these some reactionary patriots trying to stamp out ethnicity? No, curiously enough, the chief argument advanced by the proponents of the amendment is as humane as can be. Yet many readers may find it hard to see the humanity in it until they fully understand how language works. I confess that about most of the other changes in the language which I've reported here, I'm fairly relaxed— amused, sometimes; rueful, sometimes; and pleased, sometimes.

But about this issue and this one only, I'm really worried. I think we're on a wrong course in the schools, and I very much fear that while trying to do good we are instead doing great harm.

Bilingualism, as it has developed in recent years, has already had some bad consequences, if not for the entire society, then certainly for its two largest minority groups. Blacks and Hispanics who are not now masters of a reasonable approximation of a Standard English dialect, either as a second dialect or a second language or as a native dialect and language, are being condemned by bilingual education and the new bilingualism to future generations of second-class citizenship in this country. Bilingual and bidialectal programs as they generally function today in the schools, if continued as they now are and as they are planned, ensure this outcome for a great many of the members of these minority populations. We have made some serious mistakes, and the irony of it is that we are laying the groundwork for future pain and deprivation by our most earnest efforts to undo past pain and deprivation. A chief cause is our ignorance of the way languages really work.

The adjective *bilingual* has been around for more than a century, and its current meanings illustrate still more linguistic change. The *Oxford English Dictionary* has an 1862 citation for the sense "Having or characterized by two languages," as well as others as early as 1839 and 1847 with the meaning of "Written or inscribed simultaneously in parallel versions in two different languages." In the senses "the ability to speak two languages," and the "constant oral use of two languages," the *Ninth New Collegiate* reports the word's earliest appearance as 1873. Of course, no humanist could find anything but pleasure, profit, and laudable purpose in any of *these* matters bilingual. Liberal arts colleges in this country have usually urged and frequently required the study of a foreign language by anyone seeking a baccalaureate degree. Some facility with a modern foreign language has especially been desired of those entering the diplomatic service, overseas business, and a range of other careers in addition to the academic. Nearly everyone has given at least lip service to the idea that there are many benefits in the *mastery* of another language, and there is still a good deal of sentiment in support of the presumed (though often challenged) benefits of just the *study* of another language. Most teachers of the liberal arts and sciences recognize that the ability to speak, understand, read, write, and even think in a language other than our own is one mark of the cultivated, cosmopolitan citizen; conversely, many believe too that the lack of such skills identifies the provincial.

Further, many academics are certain that real facility with another language makes possible one of the most important benefits of a liberal education: the development of insight into another culture, another people, and another time and place, with such understanding that we may finally be able to imagine accurately what it would be like to be somebody else. To have that power could prepare us for acquiring wisdom. In its ideal form, then, the bilingualism of the older definitions is one of the most basic of all the tools of liberal education. I can't really imagine any serious objection to it. But keep in mind that this sort of bilingualism requires *the mastery of both our native language and one other*; it requires *equal facility in each*, not substituting the mastery of the one for the mastery of the other.

A look at the difference between *Ninth New Collegiate*'s definition of the adjective *bilingual* ("using or able to use two languages esp. with equal fluency") and the meaning of the term *bilingual education*, which the *Ninth* gives as a separate entry, immediately exposes the reason for Hayakawa's and Will's concern and mine: *bilingual education*, which the *Ninth* dates 1972, is "Education in an English-language school system in which minority students with little fluency in English are taught in their native language." That, of course, is another thing entirely. Here is no mastery whatsoever of English, even as a second language. Here, therefore, is the indefinite deferral, if not the assured denial, of the possibility that these children will ever learn the language in which most other citizens of their country speak and conduct the business of their lives and their society.

Back in the 1960s many well-meaning teachers and other citizens thought that the new bilingual education was the best way to solve two very serious problems faced by ethnic minority students whose native language was Spanish. The first problem was their falling behind in academic subjects in school because reading, writing, and arithmetic, and later on the other academic subjects as well, were all taught in English. Since after five or more preschool years of Spanish at home and in the streets and playgrounds, these pupils were now obliged first to learn English and then the various subject matters, it seemed inevitable that they must become discouraged, fall back, fail, and ultimately drop out. But bilingual education would see to it that they learned the academic materials in the native Spanish dialect they already spoke, and then later, as a secondary purpose and in a separate effort, bilingual education would bring their English up to speed. On the face of it, the proposal seemed plausible. But in fact it couldn't work unless the goal was the development of a Spanish-speaking branch of society; only one purpose—the one that seemed to be of first importance—ever got any real attention. Total immersion is the best (and for the young, almost the only efficient) way to learn a language. Learning English was clearly secondary in bilingual education programs, and in that position it was an also-ran at best.

The second problem was this: many people felt it needlessly cruel simply to toss Spanish-speaking youngsters into classrooms where only English was spoken. Not realizing that this was the fastest way to accomplish the avowed purpose—to teach them English—these people saw only apparent heartlessness and perhaps even a determination to belittle and stamp out these children's native Hispanic culture in favor of an American culture of which (some people were convinced) most of them might never really become a part anyway. To some it seemed an unnecessary deprivation which could effectively cut these children off from their parents and older relatives, who, once the children were shifted entirely to English, would (it was thought) never again be able to communicate with their offspring. Learn the new, but don't jettison the old, was the way the argument went, but it also made clear that learning the new, English, was much less important than hanging on to the old, Spanish.

George Will rejected this second argument out of hand:

> Nowadays this nation is addicted to a different rhetoric of rights—including, for a few specially entitled minorities, the right to a publicly assisted dispensation from learning the language of public life. This age defines self-fulfillment apart from, even against, the community. The idea of citizenship has become attenuated and now is defined almost exclusively in terms of entitlements, not responsibilities. Bilingualism, by

suggesting that there is no duty to acquire the primary instrument of public discourse, further dilutes the idea of citizenship. (78)

In my judgment, Will's argument has merit, but it is not the most fundamental argument against bilingual education: almost all the well-meaning claims for bilingual education turn out to be irrelevant simply because language doesn't work that way.

The reason for my intermittent concern over bilingual education during the past twenty years or so was primarily that I thought many of the evangelicals who were pushing it didn't really know much about how language is learned, and therefore I thought it likely that they had little idea of the possible damage their scheme might do. Even twenty years ago we knew a fair number of things about the way children learn language. We knew many of these things only empirically then; today we have much more basic science in hand to explain those empirical data. But we knew even then that the younger you are when you learn a language, the more quickly, efficiently, and painlessly you'll learn it. We now have a good deal of the psycholinguistic underpinning that the anecdotal evidence lacked twenty years ago. And we're learning more about these matters every day.

But even then we knew that the best way to learn a new language was to want to communicate regularly with someone who has no other language in common with us. Put the very young child in a nursery school or a kindergarten where every day he communicates with teachers and children either in the second language or not at all, and the child quickly learns the new language. And we knew too that the child never confuses the old language and the new one. To parents and siblings at home the child continues to prattle in his native language, while at school he shifts without effort to prattle in the new language. We knew that it was easy to learn French if you learned it from a French nurse-governess who spoke no English. My personal anecdotal evidence came from watching my two-to-three-year-old daughter learn Norwegian from the children and teachers at the daily outdoor nursery school she attended, while she babbled merrily away in English at home in Bergen with her Fulbrighting family. All this was known twenty years ago.

So there is one important truth that all policy involving bilingualism—the *real* stuff, not what's in the schools today—cannot ignore without harming the very youngsters it seeks to help: we must do everything in our power to introduce the second language as early as possible, the earlier the better. Nursery school is better than kindergarten, kindergarten better than first grade, and first grade better than later grades. The ideal circumstance would be to have children learn both languages at the same time, long before formal schooling begins, but since this is not a likely possibility, we must remember that the closer we can come to such a situation, the better it will be for the children. And we must not forget to saturate them in each language too. Ideally they should move from an all-Spanish to an all-English environment and then back to the Spanish again, over and over, and with no overlapping or blurred edges between them. Doling out the language learning with eye-droppered, time-paced bits from a lesson plan is impossibly inefficient, especially when teaching language to the very young.

Anything that postpones the learning of the second language for even a few months, instead of plunging youngsters in as soon and as deeply as possible, is guaranteed both to slow and to mar their acquisition of that second language. If the delay is great enough it can—and for some children it will—make total mastery of the second language (without a foreign accent, for example) impossible. This is why older youngsters and adult beginners seldom manage total mastery. And any policy that gives the acquisition of English secondary billing to arithmetic or history almost ensures that children won't ever really master it.

The argument that children who learn English in school will be cut off from their Spanish-speaking relatives is of course nonsense. Even if the child is the only one in his generation who still speaks Spanish to his parents, so long as they keep speaking Spanish to him, he'll remain fluent, even when they're eighty and he's sixty. (If they learn to talk to him in English, however broken, then of course he'll gradually lose his Spanish fluency. But so long as there is someone with whom he can communicate only in Spanish, someone he must communicate with, he'll never forget how to speak it.)

The experience of Italian-Americans in Connecticut is typical and instructive. Let's say that the great-grandparents of my student today were the immigrants, who came to the United States with their school-aged children to make a new life. The great-grandparents and their peers continued to speak Italian in their Bridgeport or New Haven neighborhood and at home, and they spoke to almost no one who didn't speak Italian. Their children, my student's grandparents, spoke Italian at home and sometimes in the homes of their friends, but in school and increasingly in the streets, they spoke English. They learned it quickly, and their parents encouraged them to do so and used them frequently to communicate with the English-speaking community. But if they were in their teens when they immigrated, as adults these children probably speak fluent but still clearly Italian-accented English today.

The third generation, my student's parents, could speak a little Italian, mostly with their grandparents and that part of the older generation they met at church and socially. But their English was wholly American, lacking any foreign flavor except in the names of foods and furniture and the processes of living in an Italian-American family. The older they became, and the fewer of the older generations there were left with whom they *had* to communicate in Italian or not at all, the rustier their Italian became. Many of them probably lost the ability to talk to grandmother about much of anything except family matters and kitchen things.

My student and her brother are in the fourth generation, the second to have been born in this country. My student can speak no Italian at all, and her brother is actually electing to study it in college. Wistfully, this generation hopes to recover some linguistic access to a culture that now, of course, they wish they knew better. That loss, of course, is the poignant argument many Hispanics use. Yet the poignancy can be a serious trap: the loss that stems from never being able truly to take part in the majority culture is greater far.

This, of course, is how the melting pot was supposed to work. And it worked pretty well for some ethnic groups: the Italians in New York and along the eastern seaboard were notable successes, and the same was true of Italians in San Francisco and elsewhere. Even though they clustered together in the cities and even though they often kept their ethnic clubs and centers, their Little Italies, and their political clout as ethnic blocs, they became or insisted that their children become Americans. Many of the later generations moved to the suburbs, went to college, and became part of the mobile society we have known since the 1930s. The linguistic "melt" opened the full range of social and economic possibilities to them.

But for other groups the "melt" either didn't occur at all or was slow and partial at best. Isolation—sometimes culturally self-imposed as with the Hasidic Jews in Manhattan or the Amish or other German sects in Pennsylvania and the Midwest, or imposed by ghetto life, as with blacks and Puerto Ricans and Mexican-Americans and other urban minorities, or set by geography, as with the Finns in upper Michigan, or the Norwegians and Swedes in rural Minnesota, Iowa, the Dakotas, and Wisconsin—sometimes slowed or totally blocked the melting process.

Religion and formal education have had an important effect on the quality of the "melting." If both these factors tended to reinforce isolation and to keep the generations closer together (some churches and synagogues and the small homogeneous neighborhood country schools often did that, as did the larger single-ethnic-group neighborhood in the big city), then the learning of English might be slowed even among the children, perhaps for almost a generation. But the breakup of religious groups or the breaking away of individuals and families, marriages outside the sect or faith, and the large consolidated school in the rural areas, like the mixed neighborhoods in the urban centers, all worked to reduce isolation and made the melting increase in both speed and efficiency.

Now, however, our largest cities have big Spanish-speaking ghettos, wherein children may hear little or no English anywhere except at school. Radio stations are Spanish-language, and so are newspapers if children happen to be fortunate enough to see one regularly. What our social situation is creating, especially in the cities, is an increased isolation, and its effect on language is prodigious, as we shall see; linguists such as William Labov interpret most of the evidence as indicating increasing, not decreasing, isolation. In a sense urban life, with its combination of economic and linguistic isolation, is forcing Afro-Americans and Hispanic-Americans to burrow more deeply into their state of hyphenated citizenship. Pride drives many of these citizens to dig themselves in still further; most seem not to realize the terrible toll this isolation will take on their children and the other generations to come.

Theodore Roosevelt made no bones about his intolerance of "hyphenated Americanism," as he called it, and it was not simply jingoism that drove him: "The one absolutely certain way of bringing this nation to ruin, of preventing all possibility of its continuing to be a nation at all, would be to permit it to become a tangle of squabbling nationalities." He chose his audience for those remarks deliberately: it was a Columbus Day speech delivered in 1915 to the Knights of Columbus in New York. Hence no one need be surprised at his later comment on the necessity for newcomers to learn the English language; George Will quotes the letter Roosevelt had read, on 5 January 1919, at something called the All-American Festival in New York: "We have room for but one language here, and that is the English language, for we intend to see that the crucible turns our people out as Americans, and not as dwellers in a polyglot boarding house."

To a modern liberal these views sound arrogant and rigid, perhaps because modern liberals' definitions of *tolerance* have been stretched and pulled into new shapes over the past twenty or thirty years. But just how far that stretching and pulling have carried us can be seen by comparing today's pluralistic tolerance with these remarks made by Henry Cabot Lodge at a meeting of the New England Society of Brooklyn, New York, on 21 December 1888: "If a man is going to be an American at all let him be so without any qualifying adjectives; and if he is going to be something else, let him drop the word American from his personal description." These are hard lines, but George Will's column explains why Lodge might well have had a point:

American life, with its atomizing emphasis on individualism, increasingly resembles life in a centrifuge. Bilingualism is a gratuitous intensification of disintegrative forces. It imprisons immigrants in their origins and encourages what Jacques Barzun, a supporter of the constitutional amendment, calls "cultural solipsism." (78)

That this hard-nosed view has at least some merit becomes clearer when measured against the way language really works. Teddy Roosevelt's "polyglot boarding house" figure is by no means silly, and his dire prediction of the disintegration and failure of the nation should the division of nationalities and their languages be permitted to go unchecked has some evidence to support it if we but look around us: at the killing, misery, and expense in operating a two-language Belgium, where universities and nearly all other social instituions have had to be duplicated to serve the French-speaking Catholics on the one hand and the Flemish-speaking Protestants on the other; at the long, painful, and expensive development of Finland, from a country divided between its Swedish-speaking and Finnish-speaking citizens, whose insistence on their differences created decades of costly political and social sparring to avoid the open conflicts of the past; or closer to home, at the anguish and folly of French-speaking Quebec and her English-speaking minorities, which have led to the whole uneasy and still unfinished business of separatism in our neighbor to the north. These are examples of debilitating, lacerating contests which no one wins.

Or consider India, where combined racial, religious, economic, political, and linguistic differences, all braided together, give each group the optimum reasons to hate the other groups within, among, or next to whom they must live. When two neighbors differ in two or more of these things, killing almost always seems to result; indeed, sometimes even one is enough. But two or three combined, as with the Sikhs in India or the Tamil in Sri Lanka, are almost irresistible. And just now the Afrikaans-speaking South Africans and the English-speaking Anglican Anglos (who have both religious and philosophic differences) appear ready to square off over the apartheid issue.

Let no one think such things can't happen here. They are already in train, although on a relatively small scale thus far. But consider the problems of the city of Miami or some of the Texas border communities. Or consider the armed camps that large areas of our older northeastern cities have become, again because language, or perhaps merely dialect differences, have coincided with ethnic or racial or religious differences. Add to that the isolation that poverty enforces, and you can understand, I think, why some people believe with Teddy Roosevelt that if the mixture in the melting pot cannot be persuaded to melt, then there is a very good chance it will explode. At the very least it seems to me clear that when close neighbors have different loyalties—*first* loyalties—to two different languages and two different cultures that seem to compete for the same powers within the same political and social jurisdictions, the situation is highly unstable.

But to see how we unwittingly permitted true *bilingualism* to deteriorate into *bilingual education*, let's turn our attention back to the late 1950s and early 1960s and to the largest racial or ethnic minority in the country—the blacks. It appears that it was from the problems many urban northern blacks faced with *bidialectism* that our troubles with bilingual education had their beginnings.

In those years, most of us had begun to be encouraged by what appeared to be improvement, after generations of stagnation and repression, in the social, political, and economic prospects for American blacks. Things seemed at last to be moving in a proper direction, albeit slowly. Education of course was in the very fore-front of the social action then, but by the mid-1960s *bidialectal education* and *bidialectism* (or, more commonly, *bidialectalism*) were undergoing the same unfortunate shift in meaning that we know developed a short time later in the meanings of *bilingualism* and *bilingual education*. *Ninth New Collegiate* defines *bidialectal-ism*, which it dates as having first appeared about 1958, as "the constant oral use of two dialects of the same language." In other words, you are master of both dialects and can slip from one to the other without effort or error. Of course, if a speaker of Northern Urban Black English can also speak (and read and write) a Standard English regional dialect from that same city—if a black South Bronx cab driver can also switch comfortably when he chooses to Mayor Koch's dialect or that of one of the WCBS radio announ-cers—then indeed in both senses of that ubiquitous modern locu-tion, there's "No problem." But for large segments of the urban black population in this country, the switch is simply not possible; their isolation has prevented them from learning a standard dialect.

Again, consider the mid-1960s. Lyndon Johnson, president from 1963 to 1969, was heavily engaged in his War on Poverty, pushing all sorts of liberal programs designed to create The Great Society. And, like improved schooling for underprivileged urban blacks, most of Johnson's programs were in a sense parts of the white majority's attempt to purge ourselves of the guilt we felt over the nation's past treatment of blacks. Meantime, the blacks' own renewed pride in self and tradition, their perceptions that "black is beautiful" and that "we need not apologize for us," set the stage for the school people to begin debating seriously whether the Northern Urban Black English dialect ought to be (1) eradicated in favor of a standard dialect that would make social mobility truly possible for its speakers, or (2) simply tolerated and pitied, or (3) adopted and "taught," as something of which to be proud, to those black children who had been reared to use it.

None of these options was as simple as it seemed. Each was emotionally loaded for all parties: guilt, arrogance, and ignorance of the way language works were spread around fairly equally. White teachers and many middle-class black teachers really didn't know what the urban black vernacular was. They assumed that because it appeared to lack certain inflections and some syntactic features that their own Standard English dialects had, it must simply be ungrammatical and hence a substandard falling off from the standard language. But they were wrong. It was and remains substandard in the eyes of the full society, but its grammar in itself is perfectly systematic and fully functional. It's just that the dialect is a vulgate system, not the standard one. These well-meaning but ill-informed teachers had confused their language and confused their sociology too. But other black people, feeling new political and social power, *at least when they operated within their own dialectal constituencies*, were determined that no one tell them that their dialect was wrong or flawed. If it's the way your mother talks, then it can't be wrong.

In the midst of contests and confusions such as these, we can readily imagine the six-year-old black child, his confidence shaken and his interest destroyed when all the signals suggest that the teacher neither understands nor approves of him, and that his language (which works fine at home and which all his role models in the family and the neighborhood speak) somehow is contemptible or wrong and won't do. His experience tells him that his language works fine everywhere he goes except in this unreal place, school. On such rocks the teaching of any Standard English dialect foundered as it was bound to do, even though it had been undertaken for the black youngster's own social good. To begin by insisting that "what you do is wrong and must be stamped out and replaced by what I do, which is right" is not effective pedagogy, particularly when the child's experience tells him that what you claim just isn't so. How much better it would have been to show him that you use *this* dialect for *this* purpose and in *these* situations, and *that* dialect for *that* purpose and in *those* situations. And above all, how much better to make him see that they're both just fine, so long as we use them in the right situations and don't get them confused. This game the child can understand; any good classroom teacher can find analogies that fit precisely the experiences of the children in a given group. And the younger they are, the easier it will be to get them interested in the game that the mastery of the new dialect can be. But that's not the way our schools approached the problem.

Next, when the first effort failed, came the idea that maybe what the schools had better do (often this was out of mistaken kindness and sympathy) was to teach those ghetto children in the dialect they already knew. As best they could, teachers would teach children to use that Northern Urban Black English dialect in speaking and in writing, for all the situations and audiences and readers they might ever encounter. Forget trying to force on them a Standard English dialect that most of them (so went the argument) will never need, anyway. Since we teachers can't possibly motivate them to want to learn it when they can't see how they'll ever need it, why make them miserable? If they do ever find themselves placed one day where they must have a standard dialect if they are to succeed, *then* they'll learn it, because *then* they'll be motivated and so can do it because they want to badly enough.

The flaws in this argument are clear enough by now: we know now, in theory at least, that if we can begin to expose children to the second dialect when they are very young, and if we as teachers know in detail the differences between their present dialect and the one we wish to teach them, so that we can instruct efficiently, then—while they're young—pleasure, not utility, can do most of the motivating. And because they are very young, in this optimum circumstance they can learn almost without strain. And the argument about waiting until they really *need* the standard dialect? We already know that any delay will make more difficulties, and that long delay can be permanently damaging. But this is all nicely theoretical. The fact remains, that if these children are to be isolated from whatever standard dialect we would have them learn, except in a classroom where only the teacher can model the new one, the task is enormous.

One of several regional models of Standard English is what the big world uses or tries to use. The written form of it is clustered around some very important central similarities in grammar and lexicon. Many blacks now speak a Standard English—more and more of them every year. As Standard English changes, they too contribute to the changing standard dialects. And with increasing confidence, numbers, time, and influence, their contribution to linguistic change and variation in the standard dialects will increase.

But here's where the problem seems to become most unmanageable. William Labov, Professor of Linguistics at the University of Pennsylvania, is one of the pioneer sociolinguists of our time, an acknowledged authority on the black English urban vernaculars. In an interview in the *New York Times* (Stevens, 14 March 1985, A14), Labov reported that recent studies make it fairly clear that urban black English dialects and the standard dialects from the same cities are diverging from each other more and more.

Once lay people hoped that television and radio would make these dialects come closer together, resemble each other more. But, Labov pointed out, "People's speech behavior . . . is not influenced by the remote communication of the mass media" (A14). And he reminded us of what language people have known for many years, that "'the primary linguistic influences are from those kinds of relationships that make a difference in your life chances,' such as those involving an employer or supervisor or co-worker." Or a teacher. Or peers and playmates, whose acceptance or rejection is so overwhelmingly important to children.

These startling points from the Labov interview in the *Times* make the nature of the problem clearer than ever before: Contact between urban blacks and whites is far less (for many blacks) than had been expected: "Many black children in broad stretches of Philadelphia almost never talk to a white person before the age of 6, when they enter school." And as the black and white dialects diverge, Labov concluded, "We're looking at this as a danger signal that our society is being split more and more, . . . and we're not ruling out the possibility that it is contributing to failure of black children to learn to read. How much a little child has to do to translate!"(A14). And the standard white dialects in big cities like New York and Philadelphia are themselves continuing to change, so that blacks and whites from the same city are encountering today an increasing difficulty in communication. As Labov put it, "in the cities, 'there's more misunderstanding between blacks and whites than any other groups'" (A14). Isolation—the social isolation of poverty and segregation however imposed, the homogenization of playgrounds, schools, churches, and streets—all these make it more difficult for some blacks ever to learn—or, until it's almost too late, even to encounter—the standard dialects of their city. Yet if we don't make it possible for black children to equip themselves with as much knowledge and experience of that standard dialect as they can and will absorb as early as possible in their young lives, we are in effect permitting them to be "tracked" for life in the ghetto just as certainly as if we refused to offer them the chance to go to school. We'll almost ensure their never being able to leave. We will have created—or at least permitted—a self-fulfilling prophecy. In that case, only the middle-class black may ever aspire to the middle class. Our goal is, I think, very clear: we must do everything in our power to give each child a real choice. We must do everything in our power too to make the choice of flexibility attractive to him.

At the moment, the schools and the programs like Head Start and others that work with preschoolers seem to be our only way even of approaching this monumental problem, with its attendant alienation and illiteracy. One thing clear is that bidialectal education is *not* the way. We've got somehow to make opportunity for the full exposure to the standard dialect these children will need, just as early in their lives as possible. Only the supremely well motivated can learn a new language as adults, and they rarely truly master it; the same goes for learning a new dialect. In some ways, as a matter of fact, new dialects may be even harder to master than new languages, for as soon as our proficiency in the new dialect enables us to understand and be understood, we have little incentive to try any further to lose those remaining seemingly trivial marks of our former dialect. This is what happens to cultivated foreigners who learn English late in their schooling or after they are adults: their English may be fluent and grammatical, but their foreign accents will still be apparent to any native speaker of English. Since they understand and are understood, as long as there is no social or professional handicap from the foreign accent, they will progress no further toward the mastery of a wholly "native" quality of English. Neither Maurice Chevalier nor Charles Boyer saw any need to improve. Nor, I guess, did Henry Kissinger. Others may have fared less well. Again, the earlier the youngster undertakes to learn that other language or that other dialect, the better.

At any rate, we did a variety of silly things in the 1960s and 1970s in the name of bidialectal education, most of them confusing to both teachers and students. What happened next was predictable. Hispanics in the West, Southwest, and Northeast, having watched the new attention the blacks had won, began to express a similar ethnic pride and a similar zeal for a better place. And again, society's response was encouraging: yes, of course we must help; and we certainly don't want to deny Hispanics their own cultural heritage. And so we began another new collection of educational programs, this time bilingual rather than bidialectal. We modeled the new ones on the bidialectal ones for the blacks, and like them, the new programs were based mainly on an imperfect view of the way language works and the way human beings learn languages.

Clearly, Hispanic-speaking upper-level grade and high school students and adults had to be met by our schools where they were. Time was a real factor. We would do the best we could, but for most of these older students, unless we could somehow learn to speed the process of learning the language, graduation from high school with their age peers who were native English speakers was simply not feasible. In fact, today still far too few Hispanics are completing secondary school, particularly if they remain essentially monolingually Spanish speaking until they enter high school. Yet our bilingual educational programs continue to involve deferral and compromise. Even preschoolers and early grade schoolers, instead of being given all-English instruction at school while they continue their native Spanish at home, divide their school time between Spanish and English, thus leaving room for doubt as to which is real. And we foster similar compromise in the adult community as well when we have the ballots and street signs and rest room labels and tax forms and the like in English *and* in

Spanish. Thus we ensure the continuation of more generations of second-class citizens, who cannot join fully in the work of the community or (as George Will puts it) in the role of citizen because they cannot communicate in the language of the majority of their fellow citizens.

Thus we build further problems for the future, as ethnicity and separateness and economics and isolation and languages all begin to reinforce each other and, among the minorities, build hatred, jealousy, and fear; then, among the majority, the recognition of these feelings in the minorities builds anger, guilt, and fear. That the contents of the pot melt* is crucial, and it is not a kindness but a cruel deception to let any non-English-speaking minority person believe that melting doesn't matter.

But how to solve the problem is less easy than it may appear to those who would amend the Constitution. I'm not quite sure about the effectiveness of the amendment. I dislike the idea of fixing things that aren't broken (like our Constitution), and I'm not certain we've taken the educational approach as far as it might carry us; it's clear we've not succeeded in helping everyone to understand how language works and therefore why bilingual education and a bilingual approach to other community problems is simply going to extend, not solve them. Being a teacher, I believe, perhaps fondly, that if people understand, they will usually do the right thing.

But Will and Hayakawa and the other amenders may be correct in their assessment of one aspect of the sociopolitical situation; perhaps they're right that we can't succeed by persuasion because our insistence on English is so certain to alienate those who will not wait to understand how language works. Maybe the position has to be legislated. In one of his most impassioned arguments, Will says:

The government has a constitutional duty to promote the general welfare, which . . . is linked to a single shared language. Government should not be neutral regarding something as important as language is to the evolution of culture. Furthermore, it should not be bashful about affirming the virtues

---

*Here's a subjunctive that only formal prose and aging writers would employ. In speech and most journalism, most Americans would expect (and say) *that the pot melts is,* or, possibly in very formal circumstances, *that the pot should melt is.* I find that I still have a fair number of these *that*-clause subjunctives, although I use them only in formal discourse and formal prose.

of "Anglo culture"—including the political arrangements bequeathed by the men of July 4, 1776, a distinctly Anglo group. The promise of America is bound up with the virtues and achievements of "Anglo culture," which is bound up with English. Immigrants, all of whom come here voluntarily, have a responsibility to reciprocate the nation's welcome by acquiring the language that is essential for citizenship, properly understood.

So, perhaps a constitutional amendment is necessary after all. My own hope is that if everyone knew and understood what I've argued in this chapter, no Hispanic or black would *permit* bilingual or bidialectal education for his children. Only for adults, for whom it's the best of bad bargains, should he entertain it. For all others, he should insist on formal education in and for the language of *full* citizenship, Standard English.

Most of the evidence argues against gradualism. The nation must hurry to correct a bad situation that appears to be growing worse. And whether my educational zeal or the amenders' amendment are tried and succeed, they will not of themselves be enough. The overwhelming, discouraging fact is the fact of isolation, because it is isolation that makes languages and dialects diverge.

Yet I see continuing trouble for the present and worse for the future if we continue as we are heading, permitting and even encouraging the evolution of a two-or-more-language society. It will cost us in every way I can think of, unless we are able to persuade majority and minority alike that it is in everyone's best interest that we teach all our youngsters as much of a standard dialect as they can master. We can reassure both Hispanics and blacks that so long as they rear their children at home during those most formative years, they will learn Spanish or Northern Urban Black English, if that's what's spoken at home, and they'll learn it without the need for schoolteachers because parents and siblings are the very best teachers of all for the pliant young. But then at school, or earlier if we can, we must make it possible for them to master a standard dialect too.

So, whether we amend the Constitution or not, do let us in any case change our bilingual policies. They have already divided us too much. We must stop using bilingual education on the coming generations, or it will do still greater harm. It may take a great deal more time and folly for such policies to run their course and (as

Teddy Roosevelt feared) destroy the nation, but it will take only a little more time and folly for them to maim her severely.*

In 1980 Dwight Bolinger published a delightful, thoughtful book on "The use and abuse of language today," to which he gave the title *Language—The Loaded Weapon*. That title has seemed to me increasingly apt as I've pondered the problems of bilingualism. Loaded weapons are of course most dangerous in the hands of those who either know nothing of guns (not even enough to fear them) or just don't know they're loaded. Our naïveté about the way language works and about what it can and cannot do seems to me to present us with a heavily ironic situation wherein, with the best and most humane of liberal good intentions, we are in the process of shooting ourselves in both feet.

The only bilingualism we can countenance is the old kind: the full mastery of both our native tongue and one other. Nothing short of that will do for any of us.

*The very recent histories of Philadelphia and Miami are frighteningly instructive on this point.

CHAPTER 15

To Hell in a Handbasket?

Edwin Newman (among others) has been telling us that unless we learn to speak and write more clearly, concisely, and honestly, and unless we cease to rely on pompous, vague, flatulent language, American society and all its institutions are going to go straight to hell in a handbasket.* Newman's gloom over the nation's future, should the linguistic fatuities he describes continue unchecked, frightens many of us. His indignation persuades us. None of us wants to be guilty of such follies. Even those of us who add daily to the accumulation of asininities Newman pillories in his books can share his pleasure in ridiculing others' gelatinous diction and silly syntax. Residents of even the glassiest houses become enthusiastic stone-throwers once a Newman has pointed out a target—even if (as Pogo used to say) "The enemy is us."

Newman is probably right about the obese language we Americans too frequently write. And he may also be right that it's getting worse. But is he correct too about the inevitable result of this dismal trend? Will our words end by destroying our institutions? And can the righteous indignation that our recognition of the truth of Newman's indictments raises in our breasts produce some change for the better?

About one thing Newman is certainly right: people get the language they deserve. The language is made by the people who use it, and they can unmake it too. If they are foolish and fatuous, their speech and writing will be foolish and fatuous and over time will shape the language itself so that it can perfectly express their folly and fatuity. But any resolve to improve this gloomy prospect

---

*"Handbasket. BASKET sb. A basket to be carried in the hand." In support of its definition, OED offers citations from 1495–97 to 1768–74. The word is not in Webster III or the Century. So far as I'm aware, the word is obsolete, preserved only in this cliché, whose origin I've not been able to trace.

poses a chicken-or-egg question which needs at least our understanding: if we work to improve the language, will we thereby also improve the shoddy values, the muddy thinking, and the trivial speakers and writers themselves? Or must we begin at the other end, trying first to improve the people, their thinking, and their values, because only after these improve will the language itself change to reflect the improvements?

Most linguists agree that every natural language adequately serves its users: it has what they need, and whatever means it may lack for perception, communication, or expression that we might find in other languages but not in this one, the users of this language do not need. If the users' needs change, then the language will change to accommodate them. On this view of the system, there is general agreement.

Whenever we attempt to break into the system in an effort to improve it, therefore, we must face the fact that sloppy-thinking, muddleheaded people will speak and write sloppy, muddled language. It will fully satisfy their needs, and for their purposes it will accurately express their values. Hence we might well conclude both that the language will not change unless its users change (for better or worse), and that if the users don't change, then the language they have formed will ensure that succeeding generations of its users will be sloppy-minded and muddleheaded like their predecessors.

I knew or suspected most of this back in 1966 when I left the study of the language and nodded off. I suspect that most students of language knew it then. But most lay people, even when they're willing to accept expert counsel on the point, just can't bring themselves to believe that these things are really in the long run the truth. The response then, and now, is, "Isn't there *anything* the teachers, the textbooks, and the dictionaries can do?" And the answer of course is more complicated than they like. Language is made by the people who use it, and these people affect the language mainly in the aggregate, even though individuals may occasionally have an impact on some aspect of a language for a brief time. As the users change (and all living societies are in constant change and variation), their language will change with them, in order that it may continue to serve all their needs for perception, communication, and expression. And since all the users of a given language are by no means alike in tastes, interests, needs, or abilities, the language must be serviceable to a considerable variety of people in a considerable variety of situations and circumstances. Most of us, the older we get, find ourselves wishing that change would slow down or go away and leave us alone or wait 'til the next generation. One of the clear lessons that my Van Winkling hiatus taught me is the importance of generational change in attitude—from the youthful zeal for change, to the middle-aged reluctance to see it, to the elderly hatred or fear of it—in nearly every aspect of linguistic manners.

On the chicken-and-egg question, only one real course of action is open to us. We cannot, by fiat or plan or rule by Academy, bring about sweeping changes in language. We cannot change even spelling wholesale; we can only nibble at the edges and tinker with the details of the language. It seems to me that in every period of its history, the English language has offered documentation of the conclusion that we have scant hope of changing or even "fixing" the language for whatever we may mean by "the better" unless and until we first change its users and their values. That, you must agree, is more than a monumental undertaking. Yet I think there is a course of action for those who will try, and I'm confident that in their contribution to the aggregate, individuals can have an effect.

The language itself, as reflected in the chambers of horrors collected by Edwin Newman and others (and some of the current examples of change I have presented here will have struck some of you as additional exhibits for such chambers), is the tangible evidence that leads reformers and other evangelicals to demand action. For some, the goal is to make the language stand still and deteriorate no further (*deteriorate* here means "change in ways I don't like"). For others the intent is to roll back the calendar and the language to a better and more nearly golden time—at least that of their youth, if not of some earlier, even finer age. (Perhaps King James's or Shakespeare's would do? Or why not Chaucer's?) Alas, neither stopping change nor rolling back the calendar and the language with it is a possible goal while the language lives; it will keep on changing so long as we use it. Nor was there really ever a golden age; what we see from here is merely the golden haze of wishful thinking, blurring the details of our vision of the past.

At every period in the history of English, there have been Edwin

Newmans—*good* men, men of taste and determination—viewing with alarm or sickened or frightened or angered by the changes and what they have seen as other signs of degeneration in their contemporaries' use of the language; they have always warned us about what they have seen as clear linguistic signs of the debasement of the nation's character and the erosion of its values, as these matters are reflected in its language. And they frequently have an effect, although never the full effect they have in mind. Rather, they call attention to the generalization that language changes; the call itself must make us examine the details.

The hot dispute over the introduction of so-called inkhorn terms (scholarly Latin loanwords that—at least at first—appeared mainly in the written language during the English Renaissance) is widely documented, both in the doctrinal writings of the combatants on each side of the issue and in the speech of several of Shakespeare's pedantic characters (such as Holofernes in *Love's Labors Lost* 4.3). The word borrowers, those gilders-of-English-with-Latin to give what they considered the rough-and-ready Anglo-Saxon lexicon the polish and "class" they felt it lacked, proposed to add a whole new "aureate diction." Those who thought English splendid just as it was fought the gilders as fops and fools, arguing for the preservation of the bone and sinew of the native stuff. Neither prevailed, of course: our language added great numbers of Latin and other scholarly words then, many of which (like *audacious* [1550], *education* [1531], and *egregious* [1578]) today seem as natural to the language as the most common of native English words; the opposition helped prevent the retention of hundreds and hundreds of others (such as *magnificate* [1598], *lubrical* [1601], and *adminiculation* [1670]).

Inkhornisms in the Renaissance, Swift's eighteenth-century fulminations against linguistic change, the British view of Americanisms over the past three centuries, the tempest after 1961 over *Webster III*, and the many issues that have produced the comments of the Fowlers, the Orwells, and the Newmans of our own time—all these illustrate the absence of universally certified golden ages anywhere in the history of the English language. We can conclude only that language will change, that some will applaud and try to hasten and assist that change, that some will condemn and try to prevent or delay it, and that still others, because they are ignorant or foolish or simply busy, will at some times imitate it and at others press on unconcernedly and thus become the targets of both the hot-eyed advocates of change and the heroic saviors of patrimony. This condition has cycled with varying frequencies and amplitudes throughout the history of the living language, wherever and by whomever it has been used.

Yet, as I've said, many—even the worst offenders against the canons of taste that the Newmans would preserve—respond favorably to the Newmans' criticisms; they earnestly promise (they say) to join crusades against bad writing and bad speaking. What then should we do? What can we do? We lack the bell-jar conditions required for a crusade in support of only the chicken or only the egg. The real world, the real language, and its real speakers don't work that way. Somehow the course of battle always outflanks our prepared entrenchments; the ground of the struggle seems always to shift. Failed efforts at establishing academies in both England and the United States for the "ascertaining" of English illustrate that point. So does the history of English and American lexicography from the seventeenth century on. All of history demonstrates the inevitability of linguistic change and variation. I may declare myself a *disinterested* judge of change rather than an *uninterested* one, only to find that some readers, especially among the unpliant young, will miss the distinction. Should I weep or swear because this is so? Will it matter which?

Perhaps we can only tinker and fight small skirmishes, not so much against change as against what we see as foolish choices among the options really available. If we grant that there are usually more fools and followers than there are wise people who can lead, then we must conclude that crusades designed to forestall all change, to stamp out all variation, or to return to some golden age must fail. Bernard Shaw and Colonel McCormick each tried hard to reform the English spelling system, but they failed, just as all the others have. The truth is that neatness may be desirable, but in language, neatness is not all, nor is it attainable by fiat. We do have a rage for order, but order in language is not logical but natural—natural to language itself. In any crusade to bring logical order to language, therefore, our rage must end in frustration.

It seems to me that what we must do is learn to tinker wisely with the language, rather than attempt wholesale reform. To tinker well, we must know the language well and keep abreast of all its changes and variations; then we must apply chiefly to ourselves and to our own use of the language such standards as we are able to derive from our awareness of what the language truly is and what we might be able to make it do for us.

To tinker well, I'd want to use my own ears and eyes for the changes in sounds and spellings, and I'd want to keep checking my impressions against the opinions of the editors of the really good, truly current college desk dictionaries. I'd be confident of my own judgment when it coincided with theirs, and in the end I would hope my confidence would grow until I would know when to decide that they had not yet caught up with a new change, or when I'd found a variation as yet unreported in their books.

To tinker well, I'd insist that I be fairly relaxed about my vocabulary in my informal speech and writing, and when I write for publication or for audiences and readers whom I do not know personally, I'd consciously try to please those audiences by choosing levels of discourse, syntax, vocabulary, and usage that would strike them all the way the little bear's chair, porridge, and bed struck Goldilocks: just right. If possible I'd try to please the entrenched elderly when I write for groups that include them, but I'd try at the same time not to come off sounding like a museum piece to the unpliant young who may be in the same group. I'd remember that one rarely wins a voter's support if one opens the appeal by kicking him in the shins and finishes it by jamming his hat down over his eyes.

To tinker well with usage of any sort, whether it's a daring new use of an old word, a smart-assed use of a show-off word, or a thoughtful self-defining use of a new word in the effort to convert without obviously preaching, I'd try to be quick, light, and restrained. The best expository prose and the best persuasive prose are usually that hardest of all prose to write, the prose that disappears so that only the ideas show through. Such prose is always simple.

So, to tinker well with my syntax, I'd keep firmly in mind this truth; more than ever the bone and sinew of English are its subjects and verbs ("Write with nouns and verbs," says E. B. White, the very best of them all, in Strunk and White, 71); anything that clutters the text so those bony nouns and sinewy verbs are smothered in fatty adjectives and adverbs must be cut away. And I'd try to avoid where I could in my finished prose those two clearest signs of a disorderly mind busy with the breech birth of an idea: noun phrases (especially ones with lots of verbal modifiers and strings of prepositional phrases tacked on) and passive voice; both show all the heavy breathing and sweatiness of birth pangs, but they have none of the cool, clean delight of the bright little idea gleaming happily in its crib.

And above all in my tinkering with language, I'd have fun, because the language is a measure of us and all our foibles and follies. I'd be perfectly resigned to the fact that nearly anything I say or write will, at some point or other, probably strike the wrong note with someone. So, if I've done my best, I'll simply try to learn from my bruises, but I will not let guilt undo me. And, because we're always testing each other, always trying to see if anyone knows what's right, I'd be prepared: when anyone asks me what it means, or how it's pronounced, I'll say it loudly and clearly, and I'll look 'em straight in the eye when I do it. There's almost nobody left who can withstand that sort of self-assurance, and the ones who can are the people I like best anyway: they think the language is fun, too.

As individuals we can at least serve and please ourselves with the language we use. In that there can be pleasure and possibly even virtue. We can let the air out of the flatulence we encounter, particularly when it is our own. In my judgment, our best hope is to bring as many of us as possible into full and conscious knowledge of the details of the language, including its patterns of change and variation and their origins and apparent causes. Only in that knowledge can we make sensible efforts to adhere to useful standards of our own making, acknowledging always that, even so, others' standards may in the end prevail. There will always be more folly than even the wise can put down, and few of the wise can ever be wise in all the hours of all their days. Most of us, wise or foolish, need only be able to ascertain whether the targets we choose are giants or windmills, and if windmills they be, need then only accept the likely results of our efforts. Whether in the long run tinkering will lead to the general use of the kind of language we deem best, we can only hope. Only time and our descendants will tell. Others and their standards will prevail if their influence and luck are stronger than ours.

One point is clear, however: whether we are parents or teachers or supervisors or editors or role models of whatever sort, we must defend and champion only that level of English of which we ourselves are masters. Only example, not precept, will prevail. That truth, however unpalatable to those who seek to know "the real rules about what's right" and to promulgate them, is the only truth: *only example, not precept, will prevail.*

I think that whatever we do accomplish will be done through tinkering. True, we may sometimes see our small successes as contributing modestly to the creation of a larger, more coherent scheme of linguistic values; the role for the lover and respecter of language is the humanist's role; it is the only effective role. Even should everyone else appear to worship at the wrong altars, the humanist, having examined both the details and the sweep of the generalizations about the whole of language, can choose his course. He can stand fast either for all the linguistic values he deems good, or for a few of those good values he thinks are most important or most valuable, or (if he prefer), only for those he sees as attainable. He may frequently find himself quite alone, and so he must never forget that his immediate effectiveness as evangelist will rest not so much on his rectitude as on his persuasiveness, not so much on his precept as on his example: the key question is, is he worth imitating? Even silly men or bad ones can be effective if they be persuasive. Even if we think this view cynical, we must accept its truth. Perfecting man and his institutions is at best a goal not soon attainable—perhaps not attainable at all, but certainly not soon. (The long, long run may offer slightly more hope, but not much, I think.) Some feel that the greatest value of that goal lies less in achieving it than in struggling tirelessly toward it, fully aware that we may never reach it. Language, since it is always changing, certainly makes that goal a moving target.

We can take comfort about our language in that although it may seem not to display much present evidence of progress toward an ideal of human perfectability, it is in fact always wholly serviceable to us. Long run or short, our language is always capable of serving all our purposes—laudable or contemptible, trivial or splendid. That's a kind of comfort. It's also an argument in favor of our careful and continuing study of our language, including both the sweeping generalizations about its changes and the details of its regional and social variations. I knew that argument when I went

Van Winkling, but my attempts to put myself in the picture again on my return have made the lesson clear anew.

That reexamination, unsystematic and informal though it has been, has also taught me something else: if our study of the language as an end in itself leads us to an understanding both of its details and of its trends, then that knowledge in turn can help us to fuller knowledge of ourselves. If even after that our folly carries us to hell in a handbasket, at least we'll know that we did not make the journey inadvertently.

Bibliography

Readers who haven't had enough or who want to get a second opinion on any of the topics discussed in this book may find this brief headnote helpful. Rather than comment on lists of titles to turn to next on each of a number of subjects, I try here simply to point out brief bibliographies and a handful of introductory essays already available. These can aim you at what to read on a given issue. For example, if you'd like to know more about lexicography, I'd suggest you read the three-page introductory essay in part 7 of Allen and Linn, *Readings in Applied English Linguistics*, 3d ed., 469–71 (all authors and works I name are listed in the bibliography); most of the books they mention contain bibliographies that can lead you further into any of a dozen aspects of dictionaries, their making, and their history.

Some of the very best annotated bibliographies (wherein you're given an idea of what's in the work and what it's useful for) appear in another collection of introductory essays on a variety of linguistic subjects: Clark, Eschholz, and Rosa's *Language/Introductory Readings*; their list and comments on pages 572–77 provide an excellent series of leads into social and regional variation, American dialects, Black English, bidialectalism, bilingualism, and the full range of the large subject of usage. Here too you can sort out the major contributions of several of the giants in these fields, including William Labov, Roger W. Schuy, the late Raven I. McDavid, Jr., and James Sledd, to name just four.

On sexism and feminists' interest in language, simple but balanced bibliographic information is a bit more difficult to find in one place. An eleven-year-old starting place is the annotated bibliography edited by Nancy M. Henley and Barrie Thorne in 1975. There is also a bibliography of about the same age in Mary Ritchie Key's *Male/Female Language*, 169–90. On avoiding sexist language, Casey Miller and Kate Swift's *The Handbook of Nonsexist Writing* presents a strong argument different in a number of ways from my own. But for the past ten years or so, the current scholarly bibliographies are almost the only completely reliable sources: the annual *MLA International Bibliography* for linguistics certainly has more about penguins than most people want to know, but it rarely misses anything worthwhile, either.

For English spelling, your desk dictionary usually has excellent descriptions and tables, but I find that chapter 3, "Letters and Sounds," in Pyles and Algeo's *Origins and Development of the English Language*, is the briefest yet most informative place to go; it ends with a short bibliography leading to almost all the major facets of writing and spelling.

Beyond these suggestions, I'd urge:

1. Buy and use the latest of good college desk dictionaries. If yours is more than ten years old, keep it, but buy a new one at once. Just now, I'd recommend either *Webster's Ninth New Collegiate* or *American Heritage II* (get both if you're a real nut on language, because they're not the same), with *Random House Revised* and *Webster's New World II* almost as good, except for their ages.

2. For the fullest story on words and their histories, there is no substitute for these three: the *OED* and its recently finished new supplement in four volumes, the Craigie and Hulbert *Dictionary of American English*, and Mathews' *Dictionary of Americanisms*.

3. For the best one-volume dictionary for Americans, *Webster III* is the one.

4. Of all the dozens of special dictionaries, I'd particularly single out these for those of you who like watching the vocabulary change: the Morrises' *Harper Dictionary of Contemporary Usage*, 2d ed., and the Barnhart, Steinmetz, and Barnhart collections of the newest words.

5. For succinct and fascinating information about your language, be sure to read the several essays and charts in the front or rear of your college dictionary. Some of these are absolutely first rate, and almost none is a waste of time.

6. Finally, read H. L. Mencken's *American Language*, in the abridged and updated edition by Raven I. McDavid, Jr. It's full of data, yet it's marvelously readable; McDavid, like Mencken, not only knew how fascinating the language is and how full of lore, but he also knew how wonderfully funny our attitudes toward it can oftentimes be. If you're interested in the language, here is surely one of the most entertaining books you'll ever read.

And here is a list of the works cited in this book and in the headnote above:

Adler, Polly. *A House Is Not a Home*. New York: Rinehart, 1953.

Allen, Harold B., and Michael D. Linn. *Readings in Applied English Linguistics*. 3d ed. New York: Knopf, 1982.

The American College Dictionary. Ed. C. L. Barnhart. New York: Random House, 1947. Mine is a 1958 printing.

The American Heritage Dictionary of the English Language. Ed. William Morris. Boston: American Heritage and Houghton Mifflin, 1969.

The American Heritage Dictionary of the English Language. College ed. Ed. William Morris. Boston: Houghton Mifflin, 1981.

The American Heritage Dictionary. 2d college ed. Boston: Houghton Mifflin, 1982.

Barnhart, Clarence L., Sol Steinmetz, and Robert K. Barnhart. *The Barnhart Dictionary of New English since 1963*. Bronxville, N.Y.: Barnhart–Harper and Row, 1973.

———.*The Second Barnhart Dictionary of New English*. Bronxville, N.Y.: Barnhart Books, 1980.

Bolinger, Dwight. *Language—The Loaded Weapon*. New York: Long-
man, 1980.
————."Usage and Acceptability in Language/For the Affirmative." In
The American Heritage Dictionary, 30–32. 2d college ed. Boston:
Houghton Mifflin, 1982.
Bryant, Margaret. *Current American Usage*. New York: Funk and Wag-
nalls, n.d. [probably 1962].
Buckley, William F., Jr. "Usage and Acceptability in Language/For the
Negative." In *The American Heritage Dictionary*, 32–33. 2d college ed.
Boston: Houghton Mifflin, 1982.
The Century Dictionary and Cyclopedia. 10 vols. Ed. William Dwight
Whitney. New York: Century, 1894–97. My copy is dated 1902.
Chaucer, Geoffrey. "Nun's Priest's Tale." In *The Canterbury Tales*. B.
4011–4636. In Albert C. Baugh, ed., *Chaucer's Major Poetry*, 371–81.
Englewood Cliffs, N.J.: Prentice-Hall, 1963.
Clark, Virginia P., Paul A. Eschholz, and Alfred F. Rosa. *Language/
Introductory Readings*. 4th ed. New York: St. Martin's, 1985.
Craigie, Sir William, and James R. Hulbert, eds. *Dictionary of American
English on Historical Principles*. 4 vols. Chicago: University of Chicago
Press, 1938.
Dictionary of American Regional English. Vol. 1, *Introduction and Let-
ters A–C*. Ed. Frederic G. Cassidy. Cambridge: Belknap Press of Har-
vard University Press, 1985.
Evans, Bergen. "But What's a Dictionary For?" *The Atlantic*, May 1962,
57–62.
Follett, Wilson. "Sabotage in Springfield." *The Atlantic*, January 1962,
73–77.
Fowler, H. W. *A Dictionary of Modern English Usage*. Oxford: Oxford
University Press, n.d.
————.*A Dictionary of Modern English Usage*. 2d ed. Rev. by Ernest
Gowers. Oxford: Clarendon Press, 1965.
Francis, C. Nelson. *The Structure of American English*. New York:
Ronald Press, 1958.
Funk and Wagnalls Standard College Dictionary. Text ed. New York:
Harcourt, Brace and World, 1963.
*Funk and Wagnalls Practical "Standard" Dictionary of the English Lan-
guage*. Chicago: J. G. Ferguson and Associates, 1943 and 1945.
Funk and Wagnalls New College Standard Dictionary. Em' ·Pha·Type ed.
New York: Funk and Wagnalls, 1956.
Guidelines on Sexism. N.p.: Prentice-Hall College Division, March 1979.
Henley, Nancy, and Barrie Thorne. "Sex Differences in Language,
Speech, and Nonverbal Communication: An Annotated Bibliogra-
phy." In *Language and Sex: Dominance and Difference*. Rowley,
Mass.: Newbury House, 1975.
Irving, Washington. *The Sketch Book*. Vol. 1 of *The Complete Works*.
Pocantico Ed. New York: G. P. Putnam's Sons, n.d.

Ives, Sumner. "A Review of *Webster's Third New International Diction-ary.*" *Word Study* 37.2 (1961): 1–8.

"Keep Your Old Webster's." Editorial. *Washington Post*, 17 January 1962, A14.

Key, Mary Ritchie. "Linguistic Behavior of Male and Female." *Linguis-tics* 88 (1972): 15–31. Reprinted in *Readings in Applied Linguistics*, 3d ed, 281–93. Ed. Harold B. Allen and Michael D. Linn. New York: Knopf, 1982.

———. *Male/Female Language.* Metuchen, N. J.: Scarecrow, 1975.

Kurath, Hans. *Handbook of the Linguistic Geography of New England.* Providence: Brown University Press, 1939.

Kurath, Hans, Miles L. Hanley, Bernard Bloch, Guy S. Lowman, Jr., and Marcus L. Hansen, eds. *The Linguistic Atlas of New England.* 6 vols. Providence: Brown University Press, 1939–43.

Lasseter, Victor. "John Le Carré's Spy Jargon: An Introduction and Lexicon." *Verbatim: The Language Quarterly* 8.4 (Spring 1982): 1–2.

Mathews, Mitford M., ed. *Dictionary of Americanisms on Historical Principles.* 2 vols. Chicago: University of Chicago Press, 1951.

Mencken, H. L. *The American Language.* 4th ed. New York: Knopf, 1945.

———. *The American Language.* 4th ed. and 2 suppl. Abr. and ed. Raven I. McDavid, Jr. New York: Knopf, 1980.

Middle English Dictionary. Ann Arbor: University of Michigan Press, 1954– . This volume is being published a fascicle at a time; it is now complete through letter R.

Miller, Casey, and Kate Swift. *The Handbook of Nonsexist Writing.* New York: Lippincott and Crowell, 1980.

MLA International Bibliography 1983. New York: Modern Language Association, 1984.

MLA International Bibliography 1984. New York: Modern Language Association, 1985.

Morris, Donald R. "Epistolae." *Verbatim: The Language Quarterly* 9.2 (Autumn 1982):3–5.

Morris, William, and Mary Morris. *Harper Dictionary of Contemporary Usage.* 2d ed. New York: Harper and Row, 1985.

Moskowitz, Breyne Arlene. "The Acquisition of Language." *Scientific American* 239.5(1978):92–110. Reprinted in *Readings in Applied En-glish Linguistics*, 3d ed, 164–80. Ed. Harold B. Allen and Michael D. Linn. New York: Knopf, 1982.

New College Standard Dictionary. Ed. Charles Earle Funk. New York: Funk and Wagnalls, 1947. My Em'.Pha.Type edition is a 1956 printing.

Newman, Edwin. *A Civil Tongue.* Indianapolis: Bobbs-Merrill, 1975.

———. *Strictly Speaking / Will American Be the Death of English?* Indianapolis: Bobbs-Merrill, 1974.

Norback, Peter, and Craig Norback. *The Awful Speller's Dictionary*. New York: Quadrangle–New York Times Book, 1974.

Oxford American Dictionary. Ed. Eugene Ehrlich, Stuart Berg Flexner, Gordon Carruth, and Joyce M. Hawkins. New York: Oxford University Press, 1980.

The Oxford English Dictionary. Compact edition. 2 vols. Oxford: Oxford University Press, 1971. This edition is the micrographically reproduced version of *A New English Dictionary on Historical Principles*. It was originally published in 10 and later in 12 vols., from 1884 to 1928. Volume 13 was the Supplement (1933), which has now been incorporated in the 4-volume new supplement (1972–86), of which I have consulted the 3 volumes published through 1982.

New Standard Dictionary of the English Language. Ed. Isaac K. Funk. New York: Funk and Wagnalls, 1963. Orig. ed. was published in 1913; rev. ed. in the years 1919, 1920, 1923, 1925, 1927, 1929, 1932, 1935, 1937, 1940, 1941, 1942, 1945, 1946, 1949, 1952, 1959.

Pooley, Robert C. *The Teaching of English Usage*. 2d ed. Urbana: National Council of Teachers of English, 1974.

Pyles, Thomas, and John Algeo. *The Origins and Development of the English Language*. 3d. ed. New York: Harcourt Brace Jovanovich, 1982.

The Random House College Dictionary. Ed. Laurence Urdang. New York: Random House, 1968.

The Random House College Dictionary. Rev. ed. Ed. Jess Stein. New York: Random House, 1975. My copy is a 1980 printing.

The Random House Dictionary of the English Language. Ed. Jess Stein. Unabridged ed. New York: Random House, 1966.

The Shorter Oxford English Dictionary on Historical Principles. 2 vols. 2d ed. Ed. William Little, H. W. Fowler, and J. Coulson. Rev. and ed. C. T. Onions. Oxford: Oxford University Press, 1936.

Sledd, James, and Wilma R. Ebbitt. *Dictionaries and THAT Dictionary*. Chicago: Scott, Foresman, 1962.

Stevens, William K. "Stronger Urban Accents in Northeast Are Called Sign of Evolving Language." *New York Times*, 21 July 1985, 36.

———. "Study Finds Blacks' English Increasingly Different." *New York Times*, 15 March 1985, A14.

Stookey, Lawrence Hull. *The Use of Inclusive Language in the Worship of the Church*. Washington, D.C.: Wesley Theological Seminary, July 1982.

Strunk, William, Jr. *The Elements of Style*. 3d ed. Rev. E. B. White. New York: Macmillan, 1979.

Thurber, James. "The War between Men and Women." In *Men, Women and Dogs*, 187–205. New York: Harcourt, Brace, 1943.

Veblen, Thorstein. *The Theory of the Leisure Class*. 1899. New York: B. W. Huebsch, 1922.

Webster's Collegiate Dictionary. 5th ed. Springfield, Mass.: G. and C. Merriam, 1936. My copy is 1941 printing.

Webster's New Collegiate Dictionary. 6th ed. Springfield, Mass.: G. and C. Merriam, 1949. I also have a 1960 printing.

Webster's New Collegiate Dictionary. 8th ed. Springfield, Mass.: G. and C. Merriam, 1973. My copy is a 1981 copyright.

Webster's New International Dictionary of the English Language. 2d ed. Springfield, Mass.: G. and C. Merriam, 1934.

Webster's New World Dictionary of the American Language. Encyclopedic ed. Ed. David B. Guralnik. Cleveland: World, 1951; New York: Simon and Schuster, 1970. My copy is 1980 printing.

Webster's New World Dictionary of the American Language. College ed. Ed. Joseph H. Friend and David B. Guralnik. Cleveland: World, 1953. My copy is 1960 copyright.

Webster's New World Dictionary of the American Language. 2d college ed. Ed. David B. Guralnik. New York: Simon and Schuster, 1970. My copy is a 1960 copyright.

Webster's Ninth New Collegiate Dictionary. Springfield, Mass.: Merriam-Webster, 1983.

Webster's Seventh New Collegiate Dictionary. Springfield, Mass.: G. and C. Merriam, 1963.

Webster's Third New International Dictionary of the English Language Unabridged. Springfield, Mass.: G. and C. Merriam, 1961. My printing is 1971.

Whorf, Benjamin Lee. "Science and Linguistics." In *Language, Thought, and Reality*, 207–19. Cambridge: MIT Press, 1956.

Will, George. "In Defense of the Mother Tongue." *Newsweek*, 8 July 1985, 78.

The Winston Dictionary. College ed. Philadelphia: John C. Winston, 1926. My copy is a 1947 printing.

Index

[Words cited as words appear in italics]